◀◀
▶ THE WEAVER'S
BOOK

THE WEAVER'S BOOK

Fundamentals of Handweaving

by HARRIET TIDBALL

Collier Books
A Division of Macmillan Publishing Co., Inc.
New York

Collier Macmillan Publishers
London

Macmillan Publishing Co., Inc.
866 Third Avenue, New York, N.Y. 10022
Collier Macmillan Canada, Ltd.

The Weaver's Book is published in a hardcover edition by Macmillan Publishing Co., Inc.

First Collier Books Edition 1976

Fourth Printing 1979

Library of Congress catalog card number: 60-13222

Printed in the United States of America

▶ AUTHOR'S NOTE

Textile technology, including its root, handweaving, is a subject with no established or generally recognized vocabulary or set of symbols. This fact occasionally creates confusion in the mind of the beginning weaver, who in reading the literature or listening to different teachers may find as many different meanings for a word as there are users of it, or several different words used for the same concept.

This is not a troublesome problem if the weaver learns one system of symbols and drafting, and one teacher's or writer's vocabulary at the outset. Then as already known concepts are redefined or different symbols are used in the literature, there is a solid foundation to which any differences may be related and therefore understood.

Several terms used in this text might well be changed to help form a more reasonable vocabulary. Most important is the word "harness" for one of the moving frames of the loom. This is a typically American word, and in time it becomes irksome to see the word always defined as a term often used by American handweavers for the word "shaft." "Harness" is the word of the handloom manufacturers, and therefore is most commonly used. But one begins to wonder if the manufacturers are suitable authorities for the establishment of vocabulary, especially when the word they use hardly makes sense and there is a much more reasonable word that is almost universally used. The word "shaft" denotes something that moves up and down vertically and therefore is more suitable for the moving frame that holds the heddles. This is suggested as a sound change that American handweavers would do well to adopt.

Another confusion of vocabulary is the present state of shift from the word "set" to "sett." In the past, "sett" has had a very specific meaning as it referred to the arrangement of different yarn colors or different yarn textures in both warp and weft. As example, the expression "Scotch tartan sett" indicated the color arrangement of both warp and weft to form a characteristic plaid pattern. The word "set" has, until recently, indicated the number of ends per inch in a warp. However, the two words have become hopelessly confused, and it is becoming increasingly common practice to use the word "sett" to cover both meanings. This is a case in which two specific meanings are lost to one general one, and is regrettable. But that is the way with language, which is never static. In this text the word "sett" is used for the noun, while the spelling "set" is retained for the verb.

For the handweaver who wishes to continue the study of handweaving through short bulletins and monographs on specialized subjects, the author of this text presents the periodical publications of the Shuttle Craft Guild. These may be secured through annual subscription. For information about the Shuttle Craft Guild write to Harriet Tidball, Route 1, Box 204B, Lansing, Michigan.

▶ CONTENTS

vii

◀◀ ▶ THE WEAVER'S BOOK

◄◄ ► INTRODUCTION

This mid-twentieth century world is a complicated place dominated by the machines which make our way of life, by the routines of profession, business or home, and by the conventions of a complex social structure. An office, a factory, a schoolroom, a home is no longer conducted through the initiative and ingenuity of the person who works in it. Machines, efficient beyond the level of human fallibility, and the ever-growing pyramid of personnel structure make the duties of everyday living continuously more routine.

But with increasing standardization and mechanization, the individual still exists as an essentially thinking and creating being. The necessity for the expression of ingenuity and for the creating of a useful product from raw materials may be removed from the home and business duties, but the ability and the desire to create remain. They demand, more insistently with some people than with others, an adequate, expressive outlet. Thus, more and more people are turning to the creative arts and crafts for fulfillment of the inherent desire to create.

Among the numerous media of creative expression: ceramics, metal-working, woodworking, silversmithing, sculpture, painting, needlework, photography, music, acting, dancing, writing, carving, basketmaking, and many others, handweaving has an honorable position. It is probably the oldest and certainly the most universally practiced of all the crafts

1

and its skills lie within the innate capabilities of most people. Textile creation may almost be called an inherent urge in the human race.

Aside from the basic reasons for wanting to take up handweaving—the desire to create, the urge to make something beautiful, the need to make something useful—there are others, such as therapeutic benefits, pleasure in the pursuit of a congenial pastime, the stimulation of sharing knowledge and experience with other weavers, and the satisfactions of gaining new knowledge and mastering new skills. These and other fulfillments accompany the activity of converting threads and yarns into beautiful, useful fabrics through the skillful use of the tools of the craft.

The person who wants to learn to weave starts by acquiring a loom and other necessary equipment, and begins immediately to use them. Without minimizing the importance of study, one may safely say that in the handcraft fields one learns by doing. With the tools at hand the student is ready to start developing dexterity in handling them, knowledge of fibers and their appropriate use, an understanding of the manner in which threads interlace to form different textile types, taste in handling problems of color selection and harmony, a grasp of the principles of good design in many styles, and judgment as to the suitability of a fabric for its purpose. The weaver works from the beginning in these six inseparable fields: mechanical skills, materials, interlacement theory, color, pattern, and function.

The ultimate objective of the weaver's desire is probably to create individual, so-called original, fabrics—that is, to design fabrics as well as weave them. Designing in a simple way may start with the first weaving through the selection of colors and materials within the limitations of the technical demands of the project. The scope of designing increases as the weaver's experience increases and as he acquires knowledge through study. But before a weaver can be truly creative, he must establish command over fundamental techniques and thread interlacement systems and develop judgment in handling fibers, color, and design. The way to develop proficiency is the same for weaving as for other arts and sciences: through copying classic models. Therefore the beginning weaver should be to a certain extent a copier.

The classic model is a well conceived design, embodying the fundamental principles of a specific weave system, combining correct materials and harmonious colors, demonstrating standards of good proportion in line and mass relationships, and altogether suited to its function. In other words, a classic model is sympathetic to the senses—beautiful. Since the classic model is a thing of beauty in itself and embodies the basic characteristics and skills of the weave system, it should be copied at the outset until the student has gained mastery over everything it can teach. After this, and only after this, the classic model may become the foundation for creating variations as dictated by the imagination of the weaver.

As the weaver's skills and knowledge increase, so also increases his respect for the work of the countless weavers through past ages. He looks with awe upon the achievements of primitive man who discovered, even before he discovered writing, the skills and techniques and designs which the modern weaver still uses. He learns to treat with great caution the word "original," as he realizes that in the weaving craft original usually means merely something which the weaver has rediscovered for his own self; uncounted people have discovered the same thing before him and are discovering it at the same time he is working. He learns that new does not mean new to the world or new to human experience, but merely new to himself. He thus gains humility and perspective and is in more sympathetic accord with the world in which he lives.

▶ THE LOOM

The loom, in its simplest sense, is nothing more than a frame to hold parallel threads, called warp, at a tension in such a way that other threads, called weft, can be woven across them to make cloth. The earliest weaving was done on a loom consisting of two sticks, one tied to an upright such as a tree and the other to the weaver's belt, between which a warp was stretched. The weaving was accomplished by picking up alternate warp threads with the fingers and placing a weft thread through the resulting division, or shed.

Early ingenuity, however, devised a system of making a shed by placing a stick across the warp with alternate threads under it, the in-between threads on top. The opposite shed was made by carrying a loop of cord around each of the down threads and then over another stick, so that raising this stick raised all the alternate warp threads. By placing weft in these two compensating sheds alternately, the weaver could produce any type of plain-weave fabric. A sword stick inserted into the sheds was used to beat the weft into its desired position. Man's innate love for decoration led to the invention of countless special techniques by which designs could be woven into the simple web. This primitive loom is still used in isolated regions of Central and South America and in other parts of the world where the tools of our more highly mechanized society have not yet supplanted those made at home.

Another form of primitive loom is used by the Navajo Indians and by carpet weavers in remote districts of southern Asia. This loom is an upright frame of vertical posts, with horizontal stretchers between them to serve as warp and cloth beams.

Some of the most amazingly intricate fabrics known have been woven on the primitive belt loom and the upright carpet loom, but for producing cloth in any quantity the primitive tools and methods are too time-consuming and require too much manual dexterity to make them practical for modern weavers. Peasant weavers the world over have used the large, treadle-operated loom with which modern weavers are more familiar. Into a framework of heavy timbers are placed a horizontal beam at the back on which warp is wound and a parallel beam at the front for rolling up the finished cloth. Above each of these rolling beams are usually plain stretchers, known as the back beam and the front beams, around which the warp and the cloth are carried. Hung in the center of the loom are two or four frames or harnesses holding heddles. These are cords or wires with eyes in the center which are suspended from top to bottom of the harness frames. Warp threads are carried through heddle eyes in planned or drafted order. The harnesses are hung exactly parallel to the warp, cloth, back, and front beams with the heddle eyes placed so that there is no distortion of the tensioned warp as it extends through the eyes from the back to the front beams. Harnesses are suspended from overhead in pairs and are tied to treadles underneath by cords extending from the bottom of the frames to the treadles; or more efficiently, both treadles and harnesses are connected to lams, which are levers lying under the harnesses and above the treadles. In a two-harness loom, when a treadle is depressed, one harness is pulled down while the other harness rises the same distance; the division of the warp threads which thus occurs is known as the shed. If the loom has four harnesses, pairs of harnesses are attached to each treadle and act together so that all sheds have two harnesses down and two up. Since there are six possible combinations of four harnesses (1-2, 2-3, 3-4, 4-1, 1-3, 2-4), four harness looms may be threaded and operated to give patterns and textures of considerable complexity. The peasant loom is also equipped with a beater suspended from overhead in front of the harnesses, which carries at the bottom a horizontal frame holding a reed through which the warp is drawn between the heddles and the cloth beam. The reed (in early days actually made of split reeds or bamboo) controls the density of the cloth by the systematic arrangement of warp ends through the dents or openings.

The peasant loom, though it must be constructed with precision, is a moderately simple tool which can be made by any semi-skilled woodworker, and it is the loom generally copied today by weavers who wish to build their own. Certain concessions to modern convenience are generally made in the use of a manufactured steel reed, steel bars in the harness frames to hold wire or flat steel heddles, and other steel parts such as ratchets and pawls on the warp and cloth beams. And with modern power tools, the home woodworker uses moderate-sized pieces of hardwood for the frame instead of the large hewn logs of the primitive model, reducing the over-all size of the loom. The bulk is further reduced if the beater is slung from the lower stretchers, as is commonly done, so that the overhead framework may be omitted.

The peasant loom, with refinements, is the common four-harness counterbalanced loom sold by many loom manufacturers today. The truly modern loom, however, is the jack loom in which each harness operates independently. There are several reasons why the modern weaver who is interested in a wide range of weaves selects the jack loom instead of the counterbalanced type. Because the independent harness action permits each harness to be suspended with absolute precision, sheds are perfect and the harness mechanism never requires adjustment. The jack operation permits more compact styling so that jack looms have less bulk; the harnesses may even be lifted from underneath, and the superstructure may thus be eliminated entirely. The jack-lifting action lends itself to the use of space-saving, exactly-fitted metal parts and to compact folding frames which are as rigid when open as the heavy square frames of yore. But perhaps the main reasons why modern weavers prefer the jack loom are that with four harnesses there are fourteen instead of six weaving sheds (1, 2, 3, 4, 1-2, 2-3, 3-4, 4-1, 1-3, 2-4, 1-2-3, 2-3-4, 3-4-1, 4-1-2); and that the looms may be extended to hold six, eight, ten, or more harnesses.

It may seem platitudinous to mention that good workmanship requires good tools; but this is as true of handweaving as of any other skill. Since the loom is the handweaver's most important tool, the weaver's first consideration is having as good a loom as he can afford to buy. There are both good and bad looms in each type and price bracket. The erroneous statement is often made that a beginner must sit at and try several looms in order to determine which one will serve him best. This is a misconception because suitability judgment can be made only after prolonged and skillful trials. The experienced weaver will select a new loom through the knowledge he has gained about the performance of looms in general. The beginner's best course is to rely on the recommendation of an unbiased, experienced weaver who has had the opportunity of using many types of looms—if such an advisor can be found. There are a few standards however by which an inexperienced weaver may compare different looms.

A loom first of all must be very strong; it should be made of hardwood throughout, as it undergoes great strain from the tension of the warp and from the vibration of the beating. The wood must be finished smoothly so that threads cannot catch. The frame must be absolutely true, with breast and back beams, warp and cloth beams, harnesses and beater in perfect parallel alignment. The shedding mechanism must open a perfect shed at least two and one-half inches wide at the reed. Counterbalanced harnesses must hang evenly, and in such a way that warp threads extending from the back to the front beams pass through the centers of the heddle-eyes. To judge the correct position of jack harnesses, stretch an unthreaded cord from back beam to front beam and raise a harness; the heddle-eyes of the harnesses at rest must be exactly the same distance below the cord as the eyes of the raised heddles are above the cord. On all looms the beater must be firm and strong, and suspended from a position as near the floor as

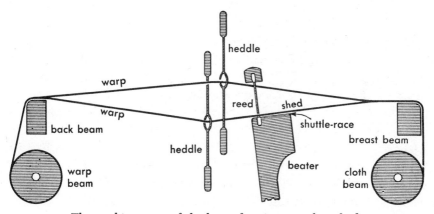

The working parts of the loom, forming a perfect shed.

possible, about half-way between the harnesses and the breast beam. It must have a shuttle-race sloped at the exact angle of the warp on the bottom half of a shed, on which the lower threads of the shed will lie smooth and with no displacement. The beater should be removable instead of permanently attached to the loom, and the reed must be easily removable from the beater. The breast and back beams of the loom, the cloth beam, and if possible the warp beam should be removable to facilitate threading.

There must be a lam hanging below each harness to which the treadle tie-up is made. There should be two more treadles than there are harnesses in a counterbalanced loom, at least four more in a jack loom. The treadles should operate lightly and responsively. A current prejudice favors front-hinged over rear-hinged treadles, but the greater leverage of rear-hinged treadles gives the loom equipped with them a lighter action, and rear-hinged treadles which are stabilized and well engineered are as convenient to operate as front-hinged ones. The distance between the beater at rest and the breast beam should be moderate, about ten or eleven inches; since the warp position must be changed every four inches or less for good weaving, regardless of the weaving space, unnecessary depth requires a longer beater each and wasted energy.

The handsomest of all looms is the push-up jack loom with no super-structure. With four or six harnesses this loom is one of the most satisfactory, but for a loom with eight, ten or more harnesses, there should be overhead jacks. In a four-harness loom one need not consider the thickness and distance apart of the harnesses, but with more than six harnesses, each one should take up a space of not more than one-half inch. The treadle-lam tie-ups are usually made with double cords, tied with snitch knots to make adjustments easy. This system is satisfactory with four harnesses, but multiple-harness looms should have efficient wire tie-ups for facilitating frequent and quick changes. Wire tie-ups never require adjustments. A well built folding loom can be as solid and strong as a rigid one, and when space and movability are considered, it is usually preferable. A counterbalanced loom should cost considerably less than a comparable jack loom. Its action is very sympathetic, particularly for a long yardage of simple design. But the person purchasing a counterbalanced loom should be aware of the fact that the limitations of the two-up-two-down harness action will eliminate any weaves which have unbalanced sheds, such as three-up-one-down. This is an extremely important consideration. People sometimes erroneously believe that a counterbalanced loom is quieter in operation than a jack loom; but a noisy jack loom is usually an improperly operated one; though it is true that in some push-up models harness clatter cannot be obviated. Whether to have wire, flat steel, or even string heddles is a matter of individual preference.

Suitable loom width is a problem which is discussed more than it deserves. The inexperienced weaver usually wants a loom of great width, but he should keep in mind the fact that shuttles must be thrown and caught. This can be a slow and difficult operation on widths greater than forty inches. Moreover, width adds bulk and operational weight to the loom as well as cost. Although many experienced weavers prefer thirty-two inch looms and find them adequate for almost all projects, if there is one universally versatile and efficient width, it is probably forty inches.

Some looms are supplied with a solid warp beam of small diameter and others with a sectional warp beam of large diameter with pegs dividing it into one-inch or two-inch sections. There is no need for discussing the relative merits of chain warping onto a plain beam versus sectional warping, as the serious weaver uses both methods according to the demands of the particular warp. Many looms are equipped with both beams; an excellent arrangement, as this also permits the weaving of double-beamed warps. But a sectional beam having smoothly rounded steel divider pegs instead of wooden ones so that it may be used for chain beaming as well as for sectional warping is the most versatile beam. The sectional beam should be three-quarters of a yard or one yard in circumference, and never smaller than two-thirds of a yard. The sections are measured from center to center of the pegs. A good friction brake is the best tensioner for a sectional beam, but a ratchet and pawl device is preferable to a poor brake.

Additional equipment required for weaving includes shuttles and bobbins with some kind of bobbin winder, a creel and a tensioner for sectional warping, a warping frame or a reel for making chained warps, and a swift for holding skeined yarns. There are many other items of equipment available which are necessary for special processes or are useful in reducing the effort or time a process requires. But the few items mentioned above are the fundamental tools which the beginner should have at once; further accessories may be purchased according to the weaver's developing inclinations.

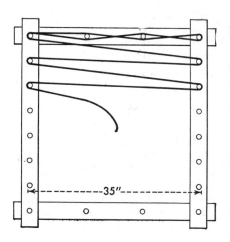

A well designed warping frame.

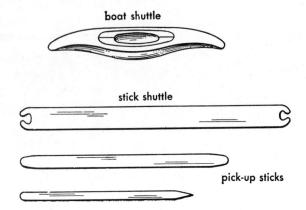

boat shuttle

stick shuttle

pick-up sticks

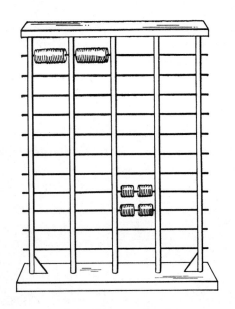

A creel or spool rack.

► YARNS

Yarns and threads in infinite variety are the materials for weaving, and the beginner has much to learn about yarns and their appropriate and effective uses. Although some basic knowledge of the characteristics of fibers is necessary at the start, significant knowledge comes only with the sensitivity to different materials which develops as the weaver handles one warp after another.

The most important textile fibers are the natural fibers: cotton, linen, wool, and silk. Commonly a beginning weaver starts with cotton, which is easy to handle. Linen and wool weaving are often erroneously considered advanced work. This idea stems from the days of handspun yarns and before good commercial yarns were available to handweavers, a situation which no longer exists. As long as the yarns used are of the best quality and intended especially for handweaving, the beginning weaver need have no apprehension about weaving with wool or linen, even as an initial project.

The "feel" and the handling of the three main fibers are altogether different and therefore it is advisable for the beginning weaver to have experience with warps and wefts of all three types as near to the beginning of his weaving career as possible. This will help develop his sensitivity to

11

fibers more quickly, and it will prevent the building up of barriers of dislike for one or another material because it is unfamiliar.

In addition to cotton, linen, wool, and silk, the modern handweaver uses a wide range of fibers both natural and man-made. The rare natural fibers are rami, jute, and hemp, all bast fibers related to linen; mohair, cashmere, angora, alpaca, and others of the minor wools and hairs; and even such oddities as woody plants, grasses, grain stalks, rattan, and raffia. Man-made fibers include rayon and acetates and the non-cellulose fibers such as nylon, dacron, vicara, orlon, and dynel, alone and in blends. Rayon is a popular and useful fiber, but the beginning handweaver will do well to avoid the newer man-made fibers. Often they are not put up in forms suitable for handweavers and most of them require special finishes after weaving which are not generally available. These fibers are so new that results are not predictable. Metallic threads, on the other hand, in their modern form are superior in quality to the old ones and are available in many exciting varieties and colors unknown to early weavers.

Cotton

For handweavers, cotton is the most widely used fiber and probably the most satisfactory. It is strong, has good elasticity, is easy to handle as both warp and weft, and comes in a generous variety of standard sizes and fast colors. Cotton may be mercerized or unmercerized. Mercerization is the treatment in caustic alkali which increases the strength of the thread, increases its dye absorption, and adds gloss. Therefore the most fool-proof material for a first warp is mercerized cotton.

Size 1 cotton has 840 yards per pound. Since the yardage increases with the size number, size 10 has 10 times 840 or 8,400 yards per pound. The cottons used by the handweaver are plied, that is, two or more strands are twisted together. Sizes are indicated by two figures separated by a diagonal line, the strand size first and the number of strands twisted together second. For instance, 10/2 cotton is two strands of size 10 yarn, 24/3 is three strands of size 24 yarn. To determine the yardage per pound of the thread, multiply the size number by 840 and divide by the ply number. Thus, size 20/2 cotton (probably the most used by handweavers) has 20 × 840, or 16,800, yards of single-strand cotton divided by 2, or 8,400 yards of thread per pound. Since the measuring is done with the single strand and there is considerable take-up in the twisting, allow for a loss of about 5 per cent when computing yarn yardage for a project.

Wool

Wool is the fiber from the fleece of the sheep and from the minor wool-bearing animals such as the cashmere goat, the mohair goat, the llama, the vicuna, the camel, and others. If the word is used without qualification, sheep's wool is meant. The wool fiber is noted for great elasticity, high luster, resilience, strength, highly insulating properties, receptivity to dyes, resistance to crushing, felting and napping tendencies, high moisture absorption, warmth, and general beauty. Wool yarns are available in three general types: woolens, which are the single-ply hand-spun type yarns; English or Bradford spun worsteds, which are the glossy, strong, crisp, smooth yarns spun from long fibers; French-spun worsteds, which are very soft, fine-fibered, dull, and strong, and are the most expensive of wools. Handweavers use English-spun worsted more than any other wool yarn, the woolen or tweeds and French-spun worsteds being appropriate for specialized textiles. Qualities and specific characteristics of yarns within each of the classes vary so greatly that generalities on them cannot be made. The weaver must learn to seek the one which will give the type of woven fabric he desires. Since woolens and worsteds require radically different processing after weaving, the two should never be combined.

Woolen yarns, usually single ply, are most commonly sized in the United States according to the Philadelphia system in which a 1-cut yarn has 300 yards per pound, and accordingly a 10-cut yarn 3,000 yards per pound, an 18-cut, 5,400 per pound, and so on. Sometimes woolen yarns are sized by the American system in which a 1-run yarn has 1,600 yards per pound, a 2-run, 3,200 yards per pound, a 2½ run, 4,000 yards per pound, and so on. There are several English count systems which differ from both of these. Woolens are carded before spinning and the fibers in the finished yarn lie in all directions instead of parallel. Dyeing is usually done before the carding. Oil is added for the spinning, and to make the yarns handle well on the loom the spinning oil is left in. Fabrics from woolen or tweed yarns must be washed or fulled after they come from the loom to remove the oil, loosen the fibers, and contract the cloth. Thus woolen yarns produce soft, opaque fabrics with a somewhat obliterated weave.

Worsted yarns, on the other hand, are made of the highest grade of wool fibers, which are processed many times before spinning to make all the fibers lie parallel. They produce crisp fabrics with clear interlacements. The English type of spinning uses the longest and glossiest fibers. Oil is added for the spinning but is removed afterward, as worsteds are dyed after they are spun. The French system uses the finest fibers, processes them more times, and spins them dry. This makes a very soft yarn without sheen but with great strength.

The worsted count system in most general use gives 560 yards per pound to a 1-count yarn, 5,600 yards to a 10-count. As worsteds are almost invariably plied, the count number is similar to that for cottons except that the ply number is placed first. For instance, 2/18 worsted means two strands of size 18 yarn twisted together to give 18 × 560, or 10,080, divided by 2, or 5,040 yards per pound. Since worsted yarns are processed so many times before spinning, the long washing required for woolen fabrics is neither necessary nor desirable for them. For the best worsted fabrics a steaming is the only processing required, though inferior worsteds benefit from a quick wash in clear, cool water.

The quality of woolen and worsted yarns determines their weavability. The handweaver should use only yarn of the highest quality. Because wool yarns cling it is necessary to weave wool warps under considerable tension, but the tension should always be released when weaving is not in progress. Wool yarns deteriorate when held on the warp beam under tension for long periods, and so wool warps should be made relatively short and woven off as soon as possible.

Linen

Linen, the "king of fibers," comes from the flax plant. It is noted for its tremendous strength and for its glossy beauty, which increases with use. As it is resistant to dyes, in the past it was used largely in natural color (gray), boiled (creamy), or bleached (crystal white); but modern dyeing now gives us many splendid linen colors. Dark and bright colors are somewhat difficult to achieve and should be color-tested before they are used in combinations. Colors do not combine well in linen fibers; so most linens are woven in solid colors.

The count system for linen gives 1-lea linen 300 yards per pound, 10-lea, 3,000 yards per pound. Plied linens are numbered like cottons, with the ply figure second. For instance, 14/2 linen has 14 × 300, or 4,200, divided by 2, or 2,100 yards per pound. Linen is spun either wet or dry, the wet spinning producing the best and most expensive yarn. It is offered as both singles, or line, linen, and plied, or round, linen; both suitable for either warp or weft if the quality is good. The beginner, however, should not risk using a singles linen finer than 12/1. The convention of weaving a ply warp with a singles weft stems from the days of hand spinning when singles yarn was too delicate for warp. On the whole, the modern weaver wishing a smooth, elegant effect will use plied linen, and wishing a textured, informal effect will use singles.

Linen fabrics must be washed thoroughly when removed from the loom. An overnight soaking and very rough washing is recommended. The more times linen is washed and ironed, the more beautiful it becomes. Linen is difficult to iron the first time, but is more tractable if the water is extracted between towels instead of by wringing. It should be ironed when wet with the hottest iron until perfectly dry, and polished after it is dry with as much pressure on the iron as possible.

Purchasing Yarns

When purchasing yarns, the beginning weaver is wise to select standard sizes and types from the sample cards of a reliable distributor who deals in yarns specifically intended for the handloom. The novelties and "glamour yarns" which come as special offerings from dealers specializing in this service are job-lot odds and ends left over from the textile mills. Although job-lot yarns are an excellent resource, they usually cannot be reordered or guaranteed in any way. The beginner is apt to have costly and disheartening experiences with them.

Estimating Warp and Weft Requirements

Before buying weaving yarns the weaver must know how much he needs of each material he is using. There is a simple formula for calculating yarn requirements:

warp width $\times$ ends per inch $\times$ warp length $=$ warp thread yardage;
thread yardage $\div$ yarn count $=$ yarn poundage for warp;
yarn poundage $\times$ 2 $=$ warp and weft requirement for any balanced weave or warp and tabby weft for two-shuttle pattern weaves.

In detail: multiply the warp width in inches by the number of warp ends per inch to determine the total number of warp ends needed. Multiply the total warp ends by the planned warp length, in yards, to determine the thread yardage needed. Convert this yardage into pounds and ounces by dividing by the figure for the size yardage given in the warp set lists, or by calculating from the count number for the particular yarn type. If the weave selected has a warp-weft balance, multiply the warp poundage figure by two to determine the total yarn requirement for warp and weft.

As an example, suppose one wishes to weave four sets of eight place mats in formal 14 inch × 21 inch size, using a balanced weave in a yarn set at 24 ends per inch. A 15-inch wide warp of 360 ends is required. With three inches allowed for hems and one inch for take-up per mat, each mat will require 25 inches of warp; 32 mats will require 800 inches, or 22-plus yards. One yard of warp must be allowed for loom waste and tie-ins, another yard for shrinkage, and the good weaver will allow one yard for experimenting. Thus a warp twenty-five yards long is planned: 25 yards × 360 ends gives a yarn yardage of 9,000 yards. If the yarn is 20/2 linen with 3,000 yards per pound, this means three pounds for warp. If it is 10/2 pearl cotton with 4,200 yards per pound, it means two pounds and two ounces. Since warp and weft are balanced in the weaving, the amount must be doubled to allow for weft too, making the requirement six pounds of linen or four and one-quarter pounds of cotton. But since the actual yarn yardage is somewhat reduced by the yarn twist and tension, there should be a safety margin. Therefore, the actual yarn order should be for six and one-half pounds of linen, or four and one-half pounds of cotton.

If the warp is to be wound sectionally the calculation is done differently. Sectional warping is preferable for a cotton warp longer than fifteen yards, particularly if the yarn may be purchased on two-ounce tubes in sufficient number to provide ends to fill one beam section. Our warp requires 24 two-ounce tubes if the beam has one-inch sections, 45 tubes if it has two-inch sections. (Notice the discrepancy here: 45 tubes instead of the expected 48. This is due to the fact that every bout (group of threads) must contain the same number of ends; so it is necessary to wind eight bouts of 45 ends each instead of seven with 48 and one with 24 to give a warp of 360 ends. The slight narrowing between the warp beam and the reed will do no harm.) To determine how many yards of warp can be wound from a set of two-ounce tubes, divide the number of yards per pound by 8 to determine the individual tube yardage, and divide this number by the number of bouts to be wound. For our cotton warp, 35 yards (safer to estimate 33) can be obtained from one set of tubes—this means that additional material has to be ordered for weft, since the warp is to be twenty-five yards long; for two-inch sections the

45 tubes would wind 63 yards of warp (safer to estimate 60)—this is adequate for warp and weft with some to spare.

Linen warps are seldom wound sectionally because they are difficult to tension adequately by this method, and because the high cost of linen inclines one to close figuring. It should also be mentioned that linen warps are seldom made as long as twenty-five yards; so this project in linen would probably be done on two thirteen-yard warps.

Warp Setts

One of the greatest problems to the inexperienced weaver—and to many experienced weavers as well—is that of determining the correct warp setting for a particular warp yarn. If there were an easy answer to this problem, weaving would be more of a craft and less of an art, as good judgment in warp setts is one of the things which distinguishes a good weaver from just a weaver. Special consideration is required for each project because the selection of warp sett, or number of warp ends per inch, depends upon the system to which the warp is to be threaded and the effect the weaver wishes to achieve, as well as upon the size and the type of the warp material. No table of warp settings is adequate. However, suggestions may be given as general guides. Three warp setts are given in the list below for each of the most commonly used cotton and linen warp sizes. For cottons, the closest or densest sett given is that suitable for twills or other single-weft weaves in which threads are raised and lowered in groups. The medium sett is that which produces a perfectly balanced tabby fabric. The most open sett is that required for two-shuttle weaves with a balanced tabby foundation and an added pattern weft.

Warp Setts for Cottons

30/2 mercerized (12,600 yards per pound) or 50/3 (14,000 yards per pound) —Twill, 45; tabby, 42; pattern, 40.
   Fine mercerized cottons, highly rewarding to the weaver with sufficient patience to work with close settings.

24/2 (10,000 yards per pound)—Twill, 40; tabby, 36; pattern, 30.
   A fine, lightweight cotton, suitable for clothing and accessories and for casements and many other household fabrics.

20/2 mercerized (8,400 yards per pound)—Twill, 36; tabby, 32; pattern, 30.
   A beautiful and very strong warp, weaving about the same as 24/2 unmercerized but with more body.

20/2 (8,400 yards per pound)—Twill, 36; tabby, 32; pattern, 30 to 27.
Probably the most commonly used cotton warp, usually set at the medium 30 ends per inch.

10/2 (4,200 yards per pound)—Twill, 27; tabby, 24; pattern, 22½.
A versatile warp especially good for beginners. More attractive in mercerized than in plain cotton. Good in heavy clothing and accessory fabrics and for decorating fabrics, particularly upholstery.

8/2 (3,360 yards per pound)—Twill, 27; tabby, 24; pattern, 20.
This is a dull soft-twist cotton of good strength, excellent for a beginning warp. The soft quality gives a greater range for good warp setts than most cottons.

10/3 (2,800 yards per pound)—Twill, 24; tabby, 22½; pattern, 20.
Usually mercerized, and one of the best warps for heavy projects. Very good for double weave and for other unusual weaves.

20/6 floss, mercerized (2,800 yards per pound)—Twill, 24; tabby, 22½; pattern, 20.
With the same weight and settings as 10/3; but this is a soft, lightly twisted yarn which gives a fabric a very different character from the other.

5/2 mercerized (2,100 yards per pound)—Twill, 20; tabby, 18; pattern, 15.
Good for heavy, specialty fabrics. Not versatile.

8/4 carpet warp (1,600 yards per pound)—Twill, 18; tabby, 15; rugs, 12.
A coarse, stiff material, useful for cotton carpets and for very coarse fabrics.

3/2 mercerized (1,260 yards per pound)—Twill, 15; tabby, 12; loose tabby, 10.
A pearl cotton, very beautiful for heavy fabrics.

The pearl, or perle, cottons have a high gloss due to gassing and heavy mercerizing. They take dyes well and are the threads which add sparkle to cotton textiles. Of all cottons they have the largest color range. In labeling, the ply number is usually omitted, but Number 20 can be assumed to be 20/2, Number 10, 10/2, and so on. Pearl floss is usually 20/6; it is very loosely twisted and therefore it flattens and covers spaces much better than 10/3 or threads of similar ply. Although heavy mercerizing makes the threads slightly smaller in diameter, the setts are approximately those for the corresponding unmercerized sizes, or slightly closer.

Warp Setts for Linens

The nature of the flax fiber permits a much wider warp-sett range than is possible for cottons. This range is greater for rough singles linens than for smooth round linens. The setts given below are for firm, medium, and open tabby fabrics: the firm tabby sett being suitable also for two- and three-thread float weaves, the medium sett for the traditional linen weaves which combine a tabby and a texture area, and the open sett chiefly for tabby and for inlay and pick-up open work. Weaves based on satin must be denser than the closest setts given here.

50/2 (7,500 yards per pound)—Firm, 45; medium, 40; open, 36.
  A beautiful linen for fine, elegant fabrics.

40/2 (6,000 yards per pound)—Firm, 40; medium, 36; open, 30.
  The standard size for medium-fine fabrics; very useful, versatile and easy to handle.

18/1 (5,400 yards per pound)—Firm, 36; medium, 30; open, 27.
  A useful size for napkins. Only the highest grade of wet-spun singles should be used. Boiled and natural types should be preferred for warp as the singles thread is weakened by bleaching and dyeing.

50/3 (5,000 yards per pound)—Firm, 36; medium, 30; open, 27.
  Notice that these setts are the same as for the finer 18/1. The reason is that the round yarn usually requires a slightly closer setting than the same size in singles; the singles will not withstand the friction of the closer warp setts.

12/1 (3,600 yards per pound)—Firm, 30; medium, 24 to 27; open, 22½.
  One of the most versatile and pleasantest linen warps to work with. In high quality wet-spun, 12/1 is sufficiently strong in both bleached and dyed yarns for good warps.

20/2 (3,000 yards per pound)—Firm, 27; medium, 24; open, 20.
  This is a standard material for medium-heavy linen fabrics. A practically fool-proof warp which is excellent at the medium sett for a first linen project.

10/1 (3,000 yards per pound)—Firm, 24; medium, 22½ to 20; open, 18.
  An excellent warp for craft linens, as it gives a beautiful texture, particularly at the medium and firm setts.

14/2 (2,100 yards per pound)—Firm, 22½; medium, 20; open, 18.
  This is a linen with considerable body, excellent for table mats.

7/1 (2,100 yards per pound)—Firm, 22½; medium, 20; open, 18.
  For less smooth textures of the same weight as 14/2.

Mercerized linen is also available in plied yarns. This is a very beautiful and very expensive yarn, desirable for the finest of table linens.

Warp Setts for Wools

Settings for wools can vary so widely that it is impossible to give even a guide. For either a woolen or a worsted fabric, the warp sett must be determined by the weaver according to the type of fabric he wishes to produce, and this must be done through sampling until a great deal of experience has been accumulated. One rule is to be remembered: a worsted is arranged at the number of ends per inch desired in the final fabric; a woolen is set considerably wider than the requirements of the final fabric because the woolen fabric is fulled or shrunk after it is woven.

All warp setts given in the above lists are based on balanced weaves, whether in tabby or in some other system. This means that they are gauged for exactly as many weft picks per inch as there are warp ends, regardless of what the warp sett may be. The achievement of this perfect balance for different warp setts, as outlined above, requires full control over the beat, the most significant command of the good craftsman.

Reed Sleys

The wide range of warp setts given in the warp sett suggestions indicates plainly that a weaver must have several reeds of different dentages if he is to weave a variety of fabrics. Probably the ideal sley for most materials is two ends per dent, though one per dent is often advantageous for very smooth yarns. But to obtain maximum value from any single reed, warps may be sleyed at three ends per dent, with one end and two ends per dent alternating, with two ends and three ends per dent alternating, or with one end in each alternate dent. Further elaboration in sley arrangements will leave reed marks in the final fabric. There is one exception to this: for very delicate yarns or for fabrics with heavy warp emphasis or warp reps, a very wide reed with a group of threads crowded in each dent is advisable. For instance, for a warp rep with sixty ends per inch one could use a 10-dent reed with six ends per dent, a 12-dent reed with five ends per dent, or a 6-dent reed with ten ends per dent.

For most weavers four reeds are sufficient, and the weaver who does fairly fine work will prefer the first four. The weaver who specializes in heavy warps will prefer a 9-dent to an 18-dent, and may prefer a 7-dent or an 8-dent to a 15-dent. Most looms come equipped with a 15-dent reed, so it is suggested that at least the 12-dent reed be ordered extra when purchasing the loom.

The table below lists seven reeds in the order of their general usefulness, with the different warp settings which may reasonably be obtained from each.

Dents per inch	Sley 1,0	Sley 1,1	Sley 1,2	Sley 2,2	Sley 2,3	Sley 3,3
12	6	12	18	24	30	36
15	7½	15	22½	30	37½	45
10	5	10	15	20	25	30
18	9	18	27	36	45	54
7	3½	7	10½	14	17½	21
9	4½	9	13½	18	22½	27
8	4	8	12	16	20	24

▶ DESIGNING

There are a few guides to over-all designing which will help the designer-craftsman produce good textiles. These are not dogmas, as exceptions to all of them exist, but they are foundations for good designing which the beginner will do well to build on. They are principles which many handweavers learn to apply slowly through trial and error but they must be grasped somehow because they make the difference between good and poor designing.

1. Simplicity is the first rule of good design. Do not confuse a design with many different ideas. The simpler the concept, the greater the chance for success.

2. Economy of means goes hand in hand with simplicity. The fewer the design elements in materials, colors, textures, patterns, the more successful the design.

3. Pick one point for emphasis. Use all the different elements of design to enhance the selected point of emphasis, allowing none to distract from it.

4. Preserve unity in composition. In other words, don't try to make a display of versatility in any single textile unless the piece is a sampler intended to illustrate many techniques.

5. Be restrained when using patterns. Use florid patterns if the func-

tion of the textile specifically calls for such, but otherwise avoid over-ornamentation.

6. A rhythmic repeat is always good design, whether one is working with patterns or with simple color stripes.

7. A rhythmic alternation of two different design elements, whether interpreted in color, texture, or pattern, gives the most satisfying results.

8. A symmetrical balance of elements lends formality to any design.

9. An asymmetrical balance of elements is more restless and gives a more vivid (and perhaps more modern) impression than strict symmetry.

10. The casual-looking design which is not based on any formal arrangement of the design elements is the most difficult to achieve effectively, and requires the greatest sensitivity to balance.

11. Pattern can be comprehended by the average eye and mind, whereas formless designs are difficult for most viewers to appreciate. Therefore, a carefully worked-out pattern will give most people, both weavers and viewers, the highest pleasurable reaction.

12. Plain surfaces, unbroken by pattern, are monotonous and likely to be depressing to weaver and viewer.

13. Patterns are emphasized by being in contrast to plain areas.

14. Odd numbers of elements compose into better over-all designs than even numbers. Three or five stripes or pattern repeats are better than two or four.

15. Avoid the use of any pattern, color, or texture plan which places a definite break or a strong emphasis across the center of an article, as this tends to divide it visually into two separate parts.

16. In setting proportions, the classical scale of two-to-three is always safe. For instance, make an oblong two parts wide and three parts long. Or divide an article into five equal parts, decorating two of these and leaving three plain, or vice versa.

17. More refined or sophisticated proportions may be determined through the use of the summation series—1:2:3:5:8:13:21:34, and so on—in which each figure is the total of the two preceding figures. This system was developed in the thirteenth century from Greek sources. The use of two or more adjacent figures gives good proportions for outlines or for groups of stripes or masses.

18. Whenever possible make a design structural by integrating the elements of color, texture, pattern, and over-all proportions, instead of adding color, texture, or pattern as superficial decoration.

19. In planning, harmonize the finishing elements with the design where possible. For instance, the hem of a table mat or a towel should be part of the over-all design.

20. Never use fringe on an article unless the fringe will actually belong to the design of the article.

21. Always be guided by the maxim, "Form follows function." The purpose for which a textile is to be used is the starting point for the designing and sets many of the limitations.

22. Every weaving technique has certain potentials and certain limitations. Select a technique because of its potentials for expressing the design idea and serving the function. This presupposes a knowledge of the characteristics of at least two techniques, though experienced handweavers have many at their command.

23. Avoid trying to design beyond the limitations of the techniques which you have already mastered. However, do not hesitate to master a new technique in order to meet a specific designing idea.

24. There are certain patterns and drafts for handweavers which have been used over and over and over. The possibility of doing something new with these is very slight, even though the articles woven on them are basically attractive. These are the trite patterns. Avoid them. Use patterns which are less commonly seen, which still retain a quality of freshness, and which still permit the weaver-designer to add something new in the interpretation.

25. An important principle is that the more complex the starting point, the less the possibility for variation, interpretation, and innovation. This applies particularly to drafts. A complex or florid threaded pattern limits the designer to a few statements, while a simple pattern-block arrangement opens up a flood of ideas for new interpretations.

26. Be concerned with expressing your own ideas and not with trying to be original. With the history of textile creation almost as long as the history of mankind, there is slight possibility that any individual can originate something which has not been known and done before. The thing the handweaver can do is to bring a fresh interpretation and a new idea to something already known.

27. Forced originality—that is, the conscious effort to do something different—will betray itself in poor designing and inadequate function.

28. As weaving experience and knowledge increase, the range of selection widens. Take full advantage of this and allow the breadth of designing to grow along with increasing skills.

Proportions for Handwoven Articles

A routine but important part of designing is knowing suitable sizes and proportions for the various articles the handweaver likes to produce. The list below will be a useful guide to correct finished sizes. It must be remembered, however, that one of the advantages of handweaving is that custom-designed articles to fit special places and unconventionally proportioned areas may be woven. One must not become so devoted to conventional proportions that freedom in designing is curbed or that an unusually proportioned custom design is considered wrong.

Afghans:	54" × 72" (may be two or three strips) 38" × 72" (may be two strips)
Baby blankets:	large crib—40" × 60" medium crib—36" × 50" or 60" small crib or carriage—30" × 42" shawls—38" × 38"
Barbecue cloths:	30" × 72", or 30" × 108" (two inches narrower than the standard barbecue table)
Bath mats:	standard—22" × 34", or 24" × 36"
Bedspreads:	double bed, floor to floor—96" × 108" (three strips) double bed, regular—86" × 108" (three strips) coverlet—76" × 100" (two or three strips) twin bed, floor to floor—80" × 108" (two or three strips) twin bed, regular—72" × 108" (two or three strips) bunk bed—60" × 90" (two strips)
Blankets:	luxury-size—72" × 90" standard double bed—72" × 84" single bed—66" × 84" utility-size—60" × 80"
Buffet scarves:	18" × 56", though seldom used now
Center runners:	14" × 28", though seldom used now
Kitchen towels:	linen tea towels—17" × 30", or 20" × 36" small glass towels—14" × 28", or 16" × 32" roller towels—17" × 96"
Napkins:	dinner—18" × 18" luncheon—14" × 14" tea—12" × 12", or 10" × 10" cocktail—5" × 8", or 8" × 8"
Neck scarves:	ascots—6" to 8" × 36" average—12" × 42" large—15" × 48" man's—14" × 50", or shorter to taste head squares—20" × 20", to 36" × 36"

Neckties:	standard bias—20″ × 30″ makes two ties
	straight ties—3″ or 4″ × 60″, piece size
	bow ties—3″ × 36″, piece size

Table cloths:	bridge—36″ × 36″, occasionally 30″ × 30″
	luncheon—40″ × 40″, or 52″ × 52″ (may be two strips)
	formal—52″ × 70″ (two strips)
	63″ × 85″ " "
	63″ × 104″ " "
	72″ × 108″ (two or three strips)

Table mats:	formal—14″ × 21″
	informal—12″ × 18″

Towels:	beach size—36″ × 72″
	luxury size—30″ × 60″
	large—24″ × 48″
	standard—22″ × 44″
	hand—16″ × 32″
	guest—12″ × 24″
	fingertip—8″ × 16″
	washcloths—12″ × 12″

Tray mats:	tea tray—15″ × 24″, or as required
	individual tray—12″ × 18″

Cloth yardages which are to be tailored should be the standard single width of 27 inches. However, the handweaver is wise to aim at 28 inches in case of selvage irregularities or weaknesses. For woolens (tweeds) the 28-inch finished width requires a 32-inch-wide warp, as about one-eighth is lost in narrowing and fulling. For correctly set worsteds a 30-inch-wide warp will be adequate as there is no fulling and there should be no shrinking in the steaming.

The average man's suit requires 7 yards of 28-inch fabric.
The average man's sport jacket requires 4 yards of 28-inch fabric.
The average man's slacks require 3 yards of 28-inch fabric.
The average woman's suit requires 6 yards of 28-inch fabric.
The average woman's full length coat requires 5 yards of 28-inch fabric.
The average woman's short coat requires 4 yards of 28-inch fabric.
The average wool shirt requires 3½ yards of 30-inch fabric.

These average requirements are all given for finished length and width of perfect fabric. Allow about one extra yard in eight for fulling loss in tweed fabrics, and about three inches per yard for take-up loss in worsted fabrics. An imperfection in the weaving of a yardage may be very costly, as a single flaw caused by as small a thing as one mistaken shed may require up to an extra yard or yard and a half for perfect tailoring. Never take yardage to a tailor unless it is perfect.

Cotton, linen, and rayon fabrics for clothing can generally be woven satisfactorily on a 32-inch warp for a final width of 30 inches. This width serves well for skirts, blouses, dresses, aprons, and anything cut from a dressmaker pattern. If a full yard width is desired, the warp should be 38 inches to 40 inches wide. Many clothing items may be made from fabrics 20 inches to 24 inches wide, if the seamstress is ingenious.

Yardages for interior decorating should be proportioned according to the demands of the project at hand. Rugs should be planned according to the rules of proportion, or as the space where the rug is to be used requires.

▶ PREPARATION FOR WEAVING

The Draft

A draft is a diagram or a system of notation which indicates the arrangement of warp threads through the heddles on the several harnesses to
form a specific texture or pattern. A pattern is any organized effect
achieved through an integrated arrangement of warp and weft threads;
a draft is a threading guide for securing the effect.

Of the many draft writing methods, one system, the *modern graphic
draft,* is becoming standard. The modern graphic draft is written on
squared paper preferably with ten spaces per inch. For a four-harness
draft four horizontal spaces are required; they should be bounded top
and bottom with strong lines. Each horizontal space represents a harness
of the loom, harness 1 (toward the front of the loom) indicated on space 1
at the bottom, harness 2 on the second space, and so on. The vertical divisions of the draft represent the warp threads. The proper harnesses from
which to select the heddles for threading are shown by the black squares,
each one placed at a point where a specific warp thread intersects a specific harness. Thus in draft 101 (page 151), reading and threading in
the conventional manner from right to left, one places the first warp
thread through the first heddle on harness 1, the second through the first
heddle on harness 2, the third through the second heddle on harness 1,

the fourth through the second heddle on harness 2, the fifth through the first heddle on harness 3, and so on. The mutual associations between threads in a pattern are thus clearly indicated at a glance. Additional aid in counting, threading, and analyzing is given by the vertical lines, which indicate each tenth thread. The conventional draft movement starts the threading on harness 1 and progresses forward to 2 rather than backward to 4 whenever possible, rather than starting on 4 and moving back to 3.

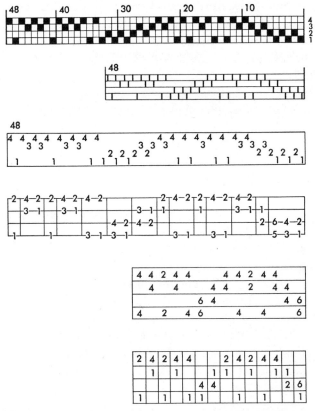

The graphic draft (top) rewritten in five different drafting systems.

A draft is properly given in entirety, but with no repeat, even for something as short as the 4-thread twill. When the end of a draft is reached, one returns to the beginning and repeats it. The inclusion of selvage threading, borders, or draft repeats indicates a specific threading schedule for a planned article rather than a generalized draft.

Other draft writing methods are significant to the handweaver who uses certain foreign publications or publications for which the drafts have been copied exactly from ancient or foreign sources without transcribing them to modern form. The preceding diagram shows a modern graphic draft and the identical draft written in five different conventions. The chance for inaccuracies and the difficulties of interpretation are obvious from a brief study of these, although it is sometimes convenient to use one of these systems when taking personal notes. Since the first draft has been literally transcribed, one characteristic of Scandinavian drafts is not revealed. This is the apparent backward motion due to the Scandinavian convention of numbering harnesses from back to front of the loom, top to bottom of the draft. A draft which seems to read 4,3,2,1, or 4,3,4,3,2,3,2,1, should be read 1,2,3,4 or 1,2,1,2,3,2,3,4 through transcription (reversal of the harness numbers) and thus set down in modern graphic convention for threading. This seemingly unimportant detail (since the weaving will be the same in the end) is of great importance to the weaver who is truly desirous of understanding drafts and textile theory and analysis. This understanding can be achieved easily only if consistent conventions are used from the beginning.

A two-block profile draft.

Another draft form is the *profile draft* used for threadings in the unit class of weaves. These weaves have perfectly stylized threadings with no overlaps, irregularities, or exceptions. In the profile draft each horizontal space represents a pattern block and each vertical space represents a static group of threads keyed to one or another weave system. The profile is thus a substitution draft requiring a key unit which is substituted for each square of the profile draft in the threading. The draft thus shows the *pattern* arrangement and proportions rather than the *threading* arrangement. (See drafts 77 through 88, pages 134–135.)

A third common draft form is the *abbreviated draft,* a type of personal notation best used as a threading guide only. In this form, groups of threads which are repeated are drafted only once and bracketed, with a figure under the draft to tell the number of times the bracketed threads are repeated. (See drafts 69, 70, 71, pages 127–129.) Although an effective short cut for threading and for writing a long draft, the abbreviated draft is not graphic, does not show proportions and relationships, and is not suitable for study and analysis of technique or pattern in most cases. One must understand it, however, as it is used as a publication form in many Scandinavian books, and often elsewhere.

The Tie-up

The tie-up of a loom is the connection made between lams and treadles to control the combinations of harnesses raised or lowered. Tie-ups vary with the type of weave to be produced, and the treadle tie-up for any special weave is indicated by a tie-up draft somewhat similar to a threading draft. The tie-up draft for a four-harness weave has four horizontal spaces, each one representing a harness, as in a threading draft. The vertical spaces of a tie-up draft indicate the treadles, and sometimes these are separated by blank spaces to facilitate interpretation. As tie-ups are read and made from left to right, the horizontal harness divisions are numbered at the left and treadle numbers progress in left to right order. The symbols in the squares indicate which harness or harnesses (by connecting the lams controlling the harnesses) should be tied to the treadle.

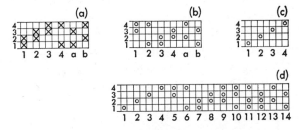

Four-harness tie-ups: (a) Standard tie-up for sinking shed. (b) Twill and tabby tie-up (standard) for rising shed. (c) Single or skeleton tie-up. (d) Full tie-up.

The *standard tie-up* draft has either x's or o's representing tie-up connections. If the tie-up is given for a sinking shed (counterbalanced loom) the tie-up is written with x's at the points where ties are made. For the rising-shed jack loom, o's are used. Tie-ups for the rare countermarch loom, in which both rising and sinking sheds must be tied and every harness is attached to each treadle, use both the x's and o's. The conversion from a sinking-shed to a rising-shed tie-up is made by putting o's into the blank spaces of the tie-up draft and leaving the x's untied, as the two shedding motions are opposite or compensating.

The simplest tie-up attaches a single harness to each of the first four treadles in 1, 2, 3, 4, order and is known as the skeleton tie-up. This tie-up is used when the shedding sequence of a weave requires the use of more sheds than there are treadles. Two or three treadles can be operated with one foot, or both feet can be used simultaneously to make a shed with two or three harnesses. The true skeleton tie-up requires six treadles, the four at the left for the single-harness tie-ups and the two at the right for the tabbies. This tie-up is not made on a counterbalanced loom, because there is no advantage; counterbalanced harnesses must be operated in pairs. Weaves which require the raising of a single harness or of three harnesses together must therefore be avoided on the counterbalanced loom unless it has a special mechanism added to force unnatural sheds. For simple twill weaving and for overshot and crackle, weaves derived from twill, the harnesses are always operated in pairs; therefore these are the weaves most commonly produced on counterbalanced looms. For these weaves the standard tie-up is used.

The standard tie-up requires six treadles for the four harnesses. Four of the treadles (those numbered 1, 2, 3, 4 starting at the left side) are tied to give pattern or twill combinations, and the two treadles at the right are tied for plain weave, or tabby. The two groups are known as the pattern treadles and the tabby treadles. To facilitate understanding the standard tie-up system, think of the harnesses as lying around a circle instead of parallel. The circle diagram shows the harnesses on the periphery of the circle. The four pattern combinations are cords between pairs

Circle diagram for determining relationships and progressions for twills and weaves derived from twills.

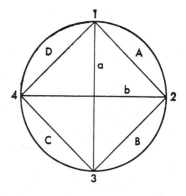

of harnesses; the tabby combinations bisect the circle. This shows that in the structure of the weave, harnesses 4 and 1 have the same mutual relationship as harnesses 1 and 2, 2 and 3, 3 and 4.

The tying of the pattern treadles at left and the tabby treadles at right permits the development of the walking-motion, touch system in treadling for weaves that alternate tabby and pattern shots, which is a requirement for good weaving. If the weaving is to be in twill order without tabby, the tie-ups on treadles 2 and 3 should be reversed so that the four twill treadles may be operated in 1, 3, 2, 4, walking-motion.

The Standard Tie-up:

Treadle 1 is tied to harnesses 1-2 (sinking) or 3-4 (rising) for combination A.
Treadle 2 is tied to harnesses 2-3 (sinking) or 4-1 (rising) for combination B.
Treadle 3 is tied to harnesses 3-4 (sinking) or 1-2 (rising) for combination C.
Treadle 4 is tied to harnesses 4-1 (sinking) or 2-3 (rising) for combination D.
Treadle 5 is tied to harnesses 1-3 (sinking) or 2-4 (rising) for tabby *a*.
Treadle 6 is tied to harnesses 2-4 (sinking) or 1-3 (rising) for tabby *b*.

Tabby combinations are always indicated by lower case letters *a* and *b* to distinguish them from pattern blocks or combinations, always shown in capitals.

Tie-ups cannot be made on a hand-operated table loom, as each harness is controlled by a separate lever. Therefore, in following treadling directions for such a loom one must substitute tie-up combinations for treadle numbers. If the tie-up is for a sinking-shed, the rising-shed conversions must be made.

Threading Schedules

A few small drafts need merely be threaded in repeats for the entire width of a warp. However, most drafts require some arrangements, adjustments, balances and the addition of selvages to fit them to the needs of a particular warp. The plan for an entire warp threading is known as a threading schedule.

The selvage is usually the first concern in the threading schedule. A selvage is an edge finish and should be as narrow as possible. Its function is to make the edges of a fabric stronger, neater, and easier to weave. It should be closely interwoven and therefore, whenever possible, it is threaded to plain weave. Because it is often more closely interwoven than the textile itself, the selvage must be narrow or its weaving will cause distortions in the body of the fabric. And because it is simply a finish and not a part of the over-all design, it should be inconspicuous. The narrowest possible plain-weave selvage is two threads to weave one-up-one-down. The best selvage width is four to six threads; anything wider than six threads should be avoided.

Certain bad selvage treatments should be strictly shunned. These are the threading of selvages with double warp ends, unless the warp is unusually fine and tender when the two-edge threads may be doubled; the use of a heavier yarn for selvages; the use of a different type of thread for selvages from that of the over-all warp. A little weaving experience will illustrate to the weaver why such practices are unnecessary and lead only to trouble.

Plain weave, threaded 1, 2 in alternation across the warp, obviously requires no special selvage threading, and there are certain other weaves for which a selvage threading is unnecessary or impossible. But most of the threadings used by the beginning weaver can be given a selvage. The selvage threading for the plain 1, 2, 3, 4 twill is merely an inversion of the two center threads to 1, 3, 2, 4 for the first and last repeats. This selvage is advantageous if most of the weaving is to be in twill, but if tabby, or plain weave, is used the selvage change should not be made.

For all weaves derived from the twill, chiefly the overshot, the hybrid and the crackle weaves, the selvage threading is twill. Special selvage threading for specific weave systems are commonly given in any analytical discussion of the system. For instance, the selvages for the Atwater lace weave are threaded 1, 2 alternately. Selvages for huck and M's and O's are threaded 1, 4 alternately. For the summer-and-winter weave there is no satisfactory selvage threading, but the close interweaving obviates the necessity for a selvage.

The next threading schedule problem is arranging the pattern elements of the draft so that they will balance and give harmony to the over-all design. This arrangement is not necessary when one is planning a simple pattern for a yardage, and it may often be avoided if the pattern is asymmetrical, but for small articles and for symmetrical pattern drafts it is very important that both sides of the design be identical. Symmetry is attained by adding a thread if the draft is a point twill, a pattern block if it is a one-motif pattern, or an entire motif if it is the more usual pattern composed of alternating motifs. The addition of blocks at each side, to accommodate to the exact number of threads in the warp or to complete a pattern motif, is sometimes a necessary part of the threading arrangement. If a border is to be added at either side, the arranging is considerably complicated, as a border which harmonizes with the pattern must be selected, the suitable border width determined, the number of repeats of the motif this width will require must be calculated, and the joining between border and pattern drafted harmoniously and identically for both sides.

As an example of the method for making a threading schedule, look at the draft given under the heading Developing Drafts on Paper, page 67.

This is selected because the development of the full draft plus a partial repeat is given, and it is only with the help of such a development that a pattern can be effectively arranged. The project for which this pattern is selected is table mats and hand towels, to be woven on a warp of 20/2 mercerized cotton set at 30 ends per inch, 14 inches wide, a total of 420 warp ends. The draft gives a simple star with a small cross at each corner. The 28 threads as they are drafted form a single-motif pattern which requires the addition of the first five threads of the draft to balance it. It has two points of symmetry, the main one at thread number 17, the center of the star, and the secondary one at thread number 3, the center of the cross. This draft could be written as two motifs by drafting the star first, threads 9 through 25, followed by the cross, threads 26 through 28 and 1 through 8.

To determine the number of pattern repeats to be used, the number of threads in the draft is divided into the number of threads in the warp: $420 \div 28 = 15$ even. This leaves nothing for the balance unit and selvages; so 14 repeats must be made and 28 threads allowed for the adjustments. First the 5-thread balance unit is subtracted, leaving 23 threads for selvages, 12 for one side and 11 for the other (there is usually one more selvage thread on one side but this irregularity is of no moment). As this selvage is too wide, it is necessary to add a pattern block at each side, which would be a B block, following the symmetry of the pattern. A 4-thread block drafted 3,2,3,2 at the beginning and 2,3,2,3 at the end would be natural, but since this would still leave an unpleasantly wide selvage it is wise to add a further block, 4,3,4, at both beginning and end, an arrangement which places the full cross at the warp edges and gives a better finish to the pattern. The schedule becomes:

Right selvage (4,3,2,1)	4 warp ends
Right balance unit (4,3,4,3,2,3,2)	7 warp ends
Pattern, 14 repeats of 28 ends	392 warp ends
Left balance unit (1,2,1,2,1,2,3,2,3,4,3,4)	12 warp ends
Left selvage (1,2,3,4,1)	5 warp ends
	420 total warp ends

Notice that the right selvage is drafted in 4,3,2,1 order and the left in 1,2,3,4 order. The direction of the selvage twill should always be the direction of the pattern blocks with which it is most closely associated. Had it been possible to start the threading at the beginning of the draft, the right selvage would have been 1,2,3,4, following the A,B,C order of blocks.

▶ DRESSING THE
LOOM

Dressing the loom means preparing the loom for weaving. It consists of winding a warp on a warping reel or a peg warping frame; transferring this warp, spread to the correct warp width, without thread twists and under proper tension, to the warp beam of the loom; threading the heddles; drawing in, or sleying the reed; tying in the warp with correct tension to the cloth beam; and making the correct treadle-lam tie-up. The only fundamental variation from this procedure is the substitution of direct beaming from spools held on a creel to a sectional warp beam for the first two steps.

The methods for accomplishing these processes must provide absolute accuracy at every stage, but otherwise they are merely means to an end, and the method the weaver selects has no significance in itself. Owing to possible variations within each process, there are almost as many ways of dressing a loom as there are weavers, and any method which produces the desired results efficiently and accurately may be considered the right one for the person using it. The beginner needs to follow an outlined method with great exactness at the outset; as warping proficiency develops he may introduce variations or short cuts to suit himself.

There is a traditional, "ancient art," warping method used without variation by many weavers, but the modern equipment used by most present-day weavers suggests different methods which are particularly advan-

36

tageous to a weaver working unassisted. By the "ancient art" method, the warp is wound on a reel or warping board with a cross, or lease, at each end. Both crosses are secured by cords before the warp is chained. A pair of lease sticks is placed through the cross at one end and the uncut ends are then drawn through a raddle, which is a 4-dent reed with a removable top; enough threads for one-fourth of an inch are placed in each dent. The lease sticks and raddle with the warp are then placed in the loom (harnesses and beater removed) and the warp beam rod is run through the uncut ends and attached to the beam. The warp is thus organized, spread, and tied in, ready for beaming. Beaming requires one person to turn the warp beam and add padding as the warp is wound onto it, and another person (or two persons) to hold the chain, organize it as it unchains by shaking or beating it or drawing the fingers through it, and keep a strong tension while the beaming is in progress. When beaming is completed lease sticks are placed in the threading cross and tied so that they hang just behind the harnesses. The threads are drawn in through the heddles, sleyed through the reed, and tied in to the cloth beam rod. The process is not as simple and easy as it may sound.

Step by step directions for a variation of this method, one which can be accomplished by one person working alone, are given below.

1. Plan the project (warp material, length of warp, width of warp, number of warp ends per inch, total warp ends).

2. Tie the warp thread around the upper right-hand peg of the warping board. Carry the thread over the first of the center pegs, under the second, and around the left peg. Cross to the opposite peg and continue around pegs on alternate sides of the board until the desired yardage is measured off. Then retrace exactly, to the top of the board. Make a cross between the two center pegs at the top by carrying the warp over the first peg and under the second. The cross will always be perfect if, regardless of the direction, the warp is carried over the first lease peg, under the second, and around the end peg. The cross should occur at about eighteen inches from the end of the warp. Continue measuring off the warp, making the cross, until enough threads are wound. To facilitate counting as one winds, separate each ten threads with a chain made of a long double strand of heavy cord. Hold the center loop around the first ten threads and pull a double loop through it. Let the ends hang down, the loop up, until another ten threads have been wound; then make a second chain around them. This chain for counting may be placed at any convenient spot on the warp and should be removed before the warp is chained off the board. Do not think it necessary to make an entire warp in one chain. It is usually easier to

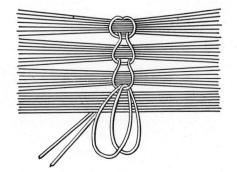

The thread counting chain.

make several small chains of 100 to 150 ends. In winding on the pegs, be sure the tension is uniform throughout, but do not make it so tight that the pegs are drawn out of line.

3. Tie a piece of heavy cord loosely through the cross between the two center pegs to hold the cross in place. Tie a cord through the loop at the end of the last peg.

The crosstie.

Chaining the warp.

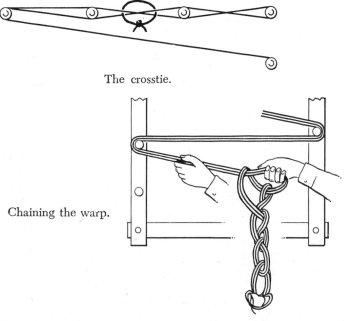

4. With the left hand, grasp the warp firmly near the lower end and slip the loop off the end peg. Place the right hand through the loop and grasp the entire warp, pulling it through to form a new loop. Put the right hand through the new loop and pull through another, continuing thus to make a chain of the entire warp, until the upper left peg is reached. Always hold the unchained portion of the warp firmly so that it will not slip over the

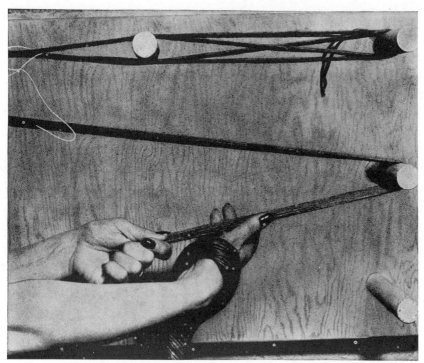

The cross is at upper left, tied with white cord.

pegs. In chaining back and forth, always face the direction of the chaining.

5. Cut the loop around the peg at the upper right-hand corner, the first peg of the warp.

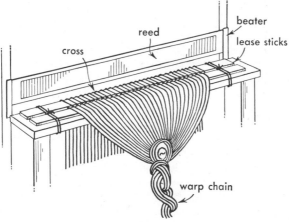

Step 6. Two lease sticks holding cross tied to breast beam.

6. Insert a lease stick or a dowel on either side of the cross as it is held by the cord. Tie both ends of the sticks firmly to the breast beam of the loom. Cut the cord holding the cross and spread the warp ends. Anchor the chain so that the warp ends will not slip out.

7. Sley the warp ends through the reed, from front to back, in the order in which the cross holds them. Be sure to measure the length of the reed and start sleying at the point which will center the warp. Draw the warp ends through the reed in pairs or singly, according to the prearranged plan. If a double sley (two ends per dent) is used, separate the paired threads in the dents, after the sleying is completed, by drawing the nearer lease stick flat against the reed and fastening it in this position. Alternate threads will thus be held up and down for easy selection.

8. Thread the heddles, working and reading the draft from right to left. Thread from back, from front, or from side of loom according to individual convenience. First push the heddles to the left side of the harness frames (be sure that there are enough heddles on each frame for the complete threading) and select a heddle at a time, pushing it somewhat to the right, threading it, and then pushing it further to the right. When ten warp ends are threaded (or more, if the pattern suggests larger groups) check them against the draft for accuracy, tie the group behind the heddles with a loop knot, and push the heddles to the extreme right. Before tying the loop, be sure the ends are all of equal length.

9. Tie the ends of the warp to the stick attached to the warp beam (this beam rod which is attached to the beam by cords or tapes must be carried around the back beam) in groups of about one inch. Use the tie-in bow, or tie with a half hitch or simple knot as desired.

10. Release the lease sticks but leave them in the warp, tying the ends together so that they cannot slip out. Unchain as much of the warp as can be stretched out at one time (five yards is a good length to handle if the space in front of the loom allows), grasp the warp firmly as far from the loom as possible, and pull it out with both hands until the tension is even throughout and all the threads are lying in order. Shaking the warp often helps organize it, but do not comb it with a comb. Draw the pair of lease sticks about eighteen inches down the warp.

11. Go to the back of the loom and turn about one-half yard of warp onto the beam, placing padding of corrugated cardboard, heavy paper, or lease sticks into the "V" where the warp goes onto the beam. Return to the front of the loom, grasp the chain and pull it very firmly to tension the warp just rolled onto the back beam. (The lease sticks, reed, and heddles have already done part of the tensioning job, but not enough.) Then pull the lease sticks down another eighteen inches, straightening the warp if necessary, and turn on another half yard. Continue thus, unchaining as required, until the shortest warp ends hang just over the breast beam. If there are ragged ends, trim them off even, but if the warp has been kept under perfect tension throughout, all warp ends will be approximately the same length.

Inserting dowels in tabby sheds to serve as tensioners.

The photograph shows an alternative and sometimes safer beaming method. Place four or six dowels into alternate sheds. Let the pair or two pairs nearest the reed be at rest to serve as tensioners and use the outer pair as warp straighteners.

12. Tie in the warp to the cloth beam rod, which has been carried around the breast beam. If using the tie-in bow, select groups of about one inch of

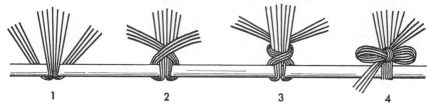

The conventional tie-in bow method. Do not tie half hitch under bow.

warp threads and tighten all groups firmly and uniformly. First tie a group at each end of the warp. Tighten the tension one notch on the ratchet. Tie a group at the center. Then tie groups at left and right, working from the center to the edges. Pull the beater halfway forward and test the tension by passing the palm of the hand gently over the warp behind the reed. If any parts of the warp are looser or tighter than the other parts, pull out the tie-in bows controlling them and retie to the proper tension.

The alternate lashing method of tie-in illustrated in the diagram and photograph is preferred by many weavers. Before starting the lashing, it is well to make a temporary tie to the left-edge group to support the cloth beam rod, and work from right to left.

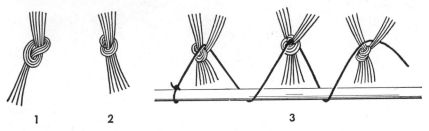

1   2   3

The lashing or lacing tie-in method. Adjust tension by pulling the cord.

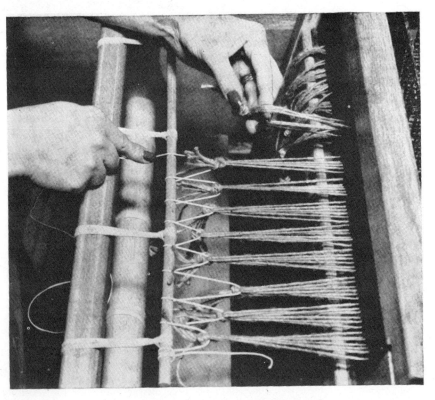

Lashing the warp to the cloth beam rod.

The loom is now ready for spreading the warp. This may be done with thread identical to the warp or with a heavy thread such as carpet warp. Open the tabby sheds alternately and throw four weft shots. Then beat these shots together, with short, sharp beats. Repeat the four shots, beating them down together, leaving loops at the edges to prevent narrowing. Probably the warp will be perfectly spread, though possibly a further repeat will be necessary. If there are no errors in the warp, weaving may now proceed.

Sectional Warping

Sectional warping, for an unassisted person the fast and efficient method of beaming a long warp with many threads, requires a creel, or spool rack, and a tensioner, in addition to a sectional beam on the loom.

The first step in sectional warping is to place on the creel exactly as many spools or tubes of warp yarn as there are to be warp ends in one

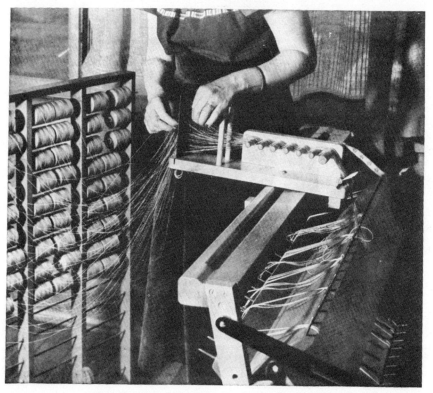

Threading the tensioner for sectional beaming.

section of the beam. (The sections of some beams measure two inches and others one inch, center to center of the pegs.) Be sure that all spools turn in the same direction. In an orderly manner, starting at the lower corner as one faces the creel, on the side of the closed end of the tensioner, and selecting each tube from bottom to top, carry each warp end, in turn, from the spool, through the collecting board of the tensioner, alternately over and under the tensioner pegs, and through the separating reed at the front of the tensioner. Arrange threads on the pegs with a cross between each two to retain order. Calculate with exactness the number of ends to place in each dent of the separating reed. When all threads have been

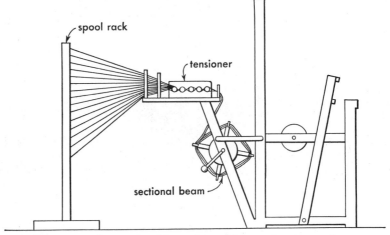

The set-up for sectional beaming with warping in progress.

entered, tie the entire group to the rod or the beam section cord at one side of the beam. Adjust the tensioner, clamped to a low table or fastened to the back beam of the loom, so that it just clears the pegs, and the ribbon of warp will turn onto the beam without catching on any pegs. Turn the warp beam the correct number of times to measure off the desired warp length. Loosen the bout slightly and, holding it between the fingers, cut it a few inches above the last pegs. Drop the ends held in the tensioner and loop the beam ends around the peg away from the position of the next bout and pull firmly. Tie the warp ribbon in position for the next section, adjust the tensioner, and wind in the same manner. Proceed in this way to fill all sections needed for the warp width. Some weavers prefer to fasten the warp ribbon in place with a strip of Scotch tape, which serves also to hold the thread order, or with a bobbie pin around the cut ends and slipped into the bout.

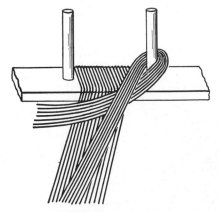

The loop to secure the warp ribbon for a single bout to a peg of the sectional beam.

To thread from a sectional beam, first remove the beater, the breast beam, and if possible the cloth beam from the front of the loom and draw a low stool directly in front of the harnesses. Loosen the warp bout at the right, carry it completely around the warp beam to give it additional length, and make final length adjustments by turning the beam. The warp ribbon must be long enough to extend around the back beam and forward eight or ten inches beyond the heddles. Hold the bout under tension to prevent any displacement of the thread order and tape it to the back beam. From the heddles which have been shoved to the left of the harnesses, select the exact number from each harness required for threading the ends in the first bout and move these toward the right. With the left hand at the left of this group of selected heddles, reach back and pick up the warp bout and hold it in a comfortable position under tension. With the threading hook in the right hand, select the correct heddle for the first thread, run the hook through the eye and back to the warp ribbon and pick off the edge thread, drawing it forward through the heddle eye. Push the heddle to the right, select the second heddle, reach through the eye with the hook, pick off the edge warp thread, and draw it through the eye. Continue thus until all the threads in the bout are through heddles. If all the selected heddles have been used by the threads, the chances are that no errors have been made, but a threading check is wise. Tie the threaded warp ends with a loop knot, push the heddles to the extreme right, select the heddles for the next bout and loosen the warp ribbon in the same manner. Some weavers prefer to unwind all bouts at the beginning and tape them securely in place on the back beam. After sufficient practice to make all motions sure and economical, this is probably the fastest threading method there is, and it proceeds very rapidly if there is an assistant to pick off each thread in order and place it in the drawing-in hook.

Threading without a cross. All warp bouts have been loosened, taped to the back beam for security, then looped around a rod suspended behind the castle.

Horizontal Reel Warping

Warping by semi-sectional method through the use of a two-yard horizontal reel attached temporarily to the loom is perhaps the fastest and easiest warping and beaming method. The method is suitable for any type of warp, plain or mixed or stripes, and for lengths up to about twenty-five yards. For this method the warper sits comfortably during the entire warping process, working alone. Beaming is merely a matter of transferring the warp from the reel to the warp beam; it is done quickly by a single person who turns the warp beam crank with one hand while tensioning the warp by putting pressure on the reel with the other hand.

Equipment required for this method is a reel two yards in circumference (usually folding) which can be attached to the breast-beam position on the loom, a tensioner secured to a weaving bench or low table, and a creel. Any number of spools or tubes of warp yarn may be used on the creel, from sufficient ends to warp one-quarter of an inch up to several inches, though the most convenient width is usually between one-half an inch and one inch. The full set-up for horizontal reel warping is shown in the photograph, the warper seated with the threaded tensioner at her right, the loom holding the reel in front, and the creel behind.

Photo from *Handweaver and Craftsman*

Winding a ribbon of tensioned warp onto the horizontal reel.

Warping is in progress. A ribbon of warp twelve threads wide from twelve tubes on the creel, carried through the tensioner, is tied to the reel's tie-in rod. The tensioner is placed close to the reel, with the warp ribbon spaced about one-quarter inch to the left of the previous bout.

After tying the warp ribbon the warper does not touch the warp again until it is time to cut the bout. The reel is turned forward, as shown in the photograph, until a sufficient number of revolutions have been made to give the desired yardage.

The photograph on page 47 shows the use of a bobbie pin to secure the warp ends before cutting the ribbon. Slip the bobbie pin around the tensioned ribbon. Release the tension a little to give some slack and insert the pin into the warp bout as shown. Cut the ribbon above the pin.

Place the warp bout in correct position by gently pushing it to the right, along each of the six reel arms, until it touches the previous bout and

Photo from *Handweaver and Craftsman*

Making the tie-in from the horizontal reel to the warp beam rod. Notice the long stick between loom arms and reel, securing the reel against moving.

fills the correct amount of space for the desired number of ends per inch. Measuring of the accumulated warp width should be done every three or four bouts as a check on the progressing warp width. This checking is facilitated if two or three plastic tape measures are cemented, with perfect precision, to the reel arms.

The photograph on page 48 is taken from the back of the loom and above, looking down into the warp. The warp is completed, the bobbie pins holding the ends are freed from the bouts, and by turning the reel sufficient warp is released to reach across the castle to the warp beam tie-in rod. A broomstick is a useful tool here. It is placed under the entire loosened warp and used to lift the warp over the castle so that the hands never have to touch or disturb it. In the photograph the broomstick may be seen where it is then placed—between the side pieces of the loom and the reel to hold the reel perfectly stationary during the tie-in. The tie-in is being made in the photograph. The lashing tie-in may be used if preferred. An edge group, still held by the bobbie pin, is picked up, the bobbie pin removed, and the bout tied to the warp-beam rod by one's favorite tie-in knot. Next the edge bout on the other side is tied, and the warp beam is tightened a notch or two. The tie-in then proceeds bout by bout either from each edge alternately toward the center or from the center alternately to the edges. Since this tie-in sets the tension for the entire warp it must be made with the same precision as the tie-in of warp to the cloth beam.

The photograph on page 50 shows the actual beaming. The warper stands at the right of the loom, removes the broomstick or whatever device has been used to hold the reel stationary, and grasps the reel with the left hand. The warp beam crank is turned with the right hand as the left hand passes from arm to arm of the reel exerting the desired tension on the warp. The process must be interrupted for inserting beam padding (sticks in the photograph) but otherwise the beaming can proceed as fast as the warper can turn the crank. If tension is never released enough to permit the warp to sag, all warp threads will pass onto the beam in perfect order. The secret of the method, if there is one, is tension.

When all the warp is beamed, gently place a stick slightly longer than the loom width under the warp and bring it up to rest across the castle. Make the reel stationary again and tighten the warp beam so that there is neither warp slack nor heavy tension. Then secure the warp to the lease stick by pressing a strip of masking tape firmly across it. The warp is now held in its beamed order and it may be cut or untied from the reel. While turning the warp beam, move the lease stick with the warp taped

Photo from *Handweaver and Craftsman*

The warp being transferred from reel to warp beam.

to it to a position just behind the harnesses and tie or clamp it there with the warp ends hanging down in the correct position for threading. A good precaution is another strip of masking tape to hold the warp to the back beam. The warp is now ready for threading.

Bobbin Winding

There are three main types of shuttles: stick shuttles for special uses, particularly with very narrow sheds or with very heavy weft; boat shuttles, which must carry a bobbin of thread and are thrown through the shed; and belt shuttles, which not only hold weft but also have a beating edge to be used for placing the weft. The usual shuttle is the boat shuttle which comes in countless types and sizes and selection is a matter of the weaver's preference. Boat shuttles require bobbins and bobbins must be wound with weft; so some sort of bobbin winder is needed. Some winders operate by hand, others by electricity. Electric winders may be bought or may be devised by the insertion of a shaft into some kind of household

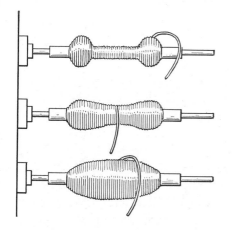

Three stages in winding a bobbin on a paper quill.

motor. The illustration shows a sewing-machine motor used for a bobbin winder. Commercial bobbins of wood, plastic, metal, or cardboard are available, but most weavers find it convenient to wind the weft on pieces of strong paper cut the proper width, called a quill.

Winding a bobbin.

Correcting Errors

With the warp beamed, threaded, sleyed and tied in, supposedly the weaver is ready to start producing a textile. Unfortunately this is often not the case. After a few shots are woven, errors in threading or sleying may become evident. It is absolutely imperative that these two steps be done with perfect accuracy; errors must be corrected at the outset. Sleying errors consist of missed dents in the reed or too many threads in a dent. If either of these mistakes occurs there is no solution but to remove the warp threads from the point of the error to the nearest edge and resley them. Sometimes a cross in the shed will appear between the heddles and the reed, preventing the formation of a proper tabby and interfering with the beating. This comes from sleying two or three threads in improper order; to correct it only the threads actually involved in the cross need be removed from the reed and resleyed in order. An error in the actual threading is more complicated to correct. The most common threading error, and one easily missed in checking, is the selecting of a heddle from the wrong harness. For instance, a tabby failure may mean that two adjacent threads lie on harness 3 when one of them should be on harness 2. The problem is solved by drawing out the incorrectly threaded warp end and rethreading it on the correct harness. But since there is no heddle available for it on the correct harness, a string heddle must be added. Make the string heddle of carpet warp. Draw it around or loop it with a

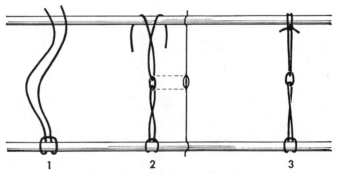

Steps in tying a string heddle.

snitch knot to the lower heddle bar. Tie a granny knot at a position exactly in line with the bottom of the heddle eyes on the same harness, lay the warp end across this, tie a second granny knot to correspond to the top of the heddle eyes, and finish by carrying the cord over the top heddle bar and tying in a granny topped with a square knot. Another common error

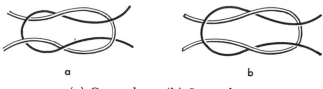

(a) Granny knot. (b) Square knot.

is due to correctly threaded ends having become twisted in the heddles. Remove the offending threads, untwist or rethread them if necessary, resley, and tie in again. Occasionally by accident two or more threads have been added to or omitted from the draft. Unless there are several omitted threads lengths of warp may be wound on bobbins, the long ends secured

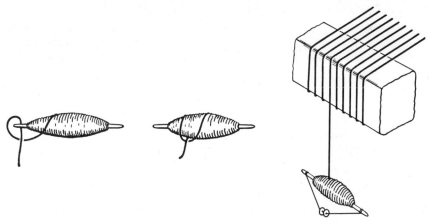

Method for inserting a correction warp end.

with half hitches, the bobbins hung over the back beam with the ends threaded through string heddles, and the warp resleyed from the point of the error. Such inserted threads are apt to be a nuisance during weaving, but their use does present a method for avoiding rethreading. Extra threads may be drawn out and the warp resleyed from the gap created. Extra unthreaded warp ends too may become a nuisance but are controlled if hung over the back beam with weights on the ends so that they cannot become tangled in the warp. Threading errors of a more extensive nature can be corrected only by rethreading.

Another source of occasional error which requires correction as the weaving progresses is broken warp ends. With a correctly beamed warp of good quality and with good weaving technique there is little excuse for broken warp threads. But accidents do happen and the weaver must be able to handle them. Remove the broken warp end from heddle and reed, tie a weight to the end of the thread, and hang it over the back beam. Wind a length of warp material on a bobbin or spool, hang the spool over the back beam and draw the end through the heddle and the reed dent. Fasten the thread end by winding it crisscross around a pin inserted just below the weaving edge, or fell. When the weaving has progressed far enough that the broken warp end may be reattached, remove the sub-

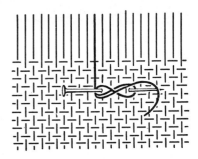

Method for fastening correction thread into fell.

stitute thread and return the original, fastening it by crisscrossing around a pin. The loose ends are carefully darned into the fabric either on the loom or after the fabric is cut off. Occasionally one may simply tie on a length of thread to extend a broken end; but knots are generally undesirable as they are apt to break in the reed, even though they can be cut out and darned over later.

Tie-up and Loom Adjustments

The tie-up is made according to the tie-up draft for the threaded weave. If the draft is twill, overshot or crackle, the standard tie-up is used. Tie-up connections in the best jack looms are made with foolproof wire systems which require only a few seconds to connect and need no adjusting after being attached. Tie-ups of cords are satisfactory if two cords are used, one attached to the lam and the other to the treadle, the loop of one and the two free ends of the other to be joined by a snitch knot. Cord tie-ups are somewhat laborious to attach and adjust, but the effort is reduced by the use of the snitch knot. If the loom is an old-style counterbalanced one, harness cord adjustments must be made along with the tie-ups to assure that all harnesses operate evenly and with precision.

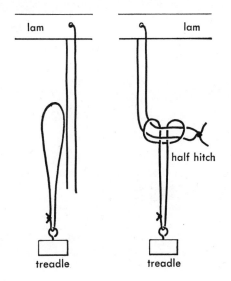

The cord tie-up.

◀◀ ▶ WEAVING

The mechanical processes of weaving are soon mastered, though skillful operation is developed only with time and practice and careful attention to correct form from the beginning. Weaving tabby is the start. Tabby is woven on two opposite sheds, each of which raises alternate warp threads. With the shuttle in the left hand, depress the *a* tabby treadle, beat, throw the shuttle from left to right, beat, depress the *b* tabby treadle, beat, throw the shuttle from right to left, beat; repeat continuously. The motions are all simple, relaxed, and rhythmic when the operation is skillful. Since weaving perfect tabby requires the placing of exactly as many weft shots per inch as there are warp ends, the force of the beat must be adjusted to achieve this warp-weft balance.

Adjusting the Warp

For most looms the weaving line for the maximum weaving space falls about two and one-half inches from the inside edge of the breast beam. To adjust the warp, rest the beater against the weaving surface, release the tension on the cloth beam, then release the catch on the warp beam, and roll up the cloth until the beater just clears the breast beam. Regardless of the depth of the weaving space, only about four inches can be woven perfectly between warp adjustments.

Warp Tension

Different types of warp require different tensions. Fuzzy or sticky materials such as wool or singles linen require a rather severe tension to force sheds apart. Elastic materials such as most cottons may be woven at a fairly loose, resilient tension. Inelastic materials like linen require sufficient tension to prevent sag. Too severe a tension puts an undesirable and unnecessary strain on the loom, the warp, and the weaver. The heavier the tension the greater is the force required to depress the treadles; the treadle action should be as light as possible. As the weaving surface progresses from the breast beam toward the beater, the angle of the shed increases and the warp is taken up in the weaving, so that the tension of the warp increases. To obviate this, as soon as the treadles become noticeably heavier, the catch on the cloth beam should be released one notch. Inability to weave a perfect tabby on a correctly set warp often means too tight a warp tension.

Throwing the Shuttle

The shuttle should be thrown on the shuttle-race with a rhythmic motion, with neither the hands nor the shuttle touching the raised warp threads at either edge. The shuttle is held lightly in such a manner that the forefinger can be used to slow or stop the spinning of the bobbin when it is caught. Different weavers hold the shuttle in different positions; it need only be said that the grasp should be natural for both throwing and catching. The shuttle when caught should be pulled far enough beyond the arc of the beater so that the weft will lie on a loose diagonal in the shed. Allow no tension on the weft during the beat. Economize motion as much as possible. Except when weaving with two or more shuttles, avoid bringing the hands toward the body; that is, keep the arms extended so that the hands are in a position to throw the shuttle along the shuttle-race and then move to the beater in a line almost parallel to the front of the body.

Two-Shuttle Weaving

The handling of the shuttle is more complicated for pattern weaving with two shuttles carrying different types of thread. The basis of most of the two-shuttle weaves is tabby; so one shuttle carries weft like the warp, while the other shuttle carries heavier pattern weft. The pattern treadles are operated with the left foot and the tabby treadles with the right, in walking rhythm. First depress treadle *a,* beat, throw the tabby from left

Correct warp and weft positions for the beat.

to right, beat, change the shed, beat, depress the pattern treadle, beat, throw the pattern weft from left to right, beat, depress tabby treadle *b,* beat, throw tabby weft from right to left, beat, depress the pattern treadle, beat, throw the pattern shuttle from right to left, beat; repeat continuously. Sometimes the beat following the shed opening may be omitted. The pattern weft follows the tabby, and in the same direction. Neat edges are made by locking the two wefts at the selvages. The lock is accomplished by always laying the shuttles down in the same relationship: the tabby shuttle toward the weaver and the pattern shuttle toward the beater, or vice versa, as long as the system is consistent. For classic pattern weaving the beat must be so adjusted that the final textile has a balanced tabby background.

The Beat

The force of the beat is determined by the weight of the beater and the speed with which it hits the fell, not by the amount of muscular force applied. Always grasp the beater exactly in the center, never at the side. Grasp it lightly so that it swings almost freely between the fingers and the thumb. Swing the beater with wrist and elbow motion, not with shoulder motion. Control the strength of the beat through the sharpness with which the beater is swung. A pair of short, sharp beats is more effective than a beat made with a great deal of muscle. No rules for "the correct beat" can be given because each different situation requires a different beat touch. Factors which influence the beat touch are type of warp material, system of threading, warp sett, warp width, warp tension, and perhaps most important—the effect the weaver wishes to achieve. A large proportion of weaves are balanced and require that the beat be perfectly adjusted to give exactly as many weft ends per inch as there are warp ends. The weaver must experiment for each new problem to discover how to beat in order to place the weft exactly as the textile requires. The beat may be a pair of short, sharp taps or a single tap; it may be made before the shed is changed, both before and after, or at the exact instant of the shed change; in fabrics for which the weft must be spaced rather widely it may even be made on a closed shed. The tap before the shed change lays the loose weft into position and presses down the previous weft. The tap after the shed change gives additional packing and clears the shed if the warp yarn is sticky. Beating only after the shed change is not advisable because it places tension on the weft and may strain the warp.

Selvages

Good selvages are not the result of careful adjustment of the weft after each shot, or of fingering or of pulling the selvage edges. Good selvages result from good weaving techniques: correct warp tension, properly wound bobbin, correct shuttle throwing, rhythmic weaving, and above all the developing of a "feel" for the warp as the reed slides through it. Therefore the making of good selvages is not the primary concern of the beginner. If the beginner concentrates on perfecting the weaving skills mentioned above, he will find that his selvages improve as his technique improves.

A strong selvage is important in any fabric not intended for cutting. This edge strength is achieved by a smooth weft-turning which is sharp, neither leaving a loop nor drawing in at the fabric edge. A few edge threads may be drawn to lie closer together than the warp sett, but the draw-in should not be more than one-fourth of an inch.

Undue narrowing of the fabric is seldom a selvage problem. It is usually due to too heavy a warp tension or to tension on the weft during the beat, or to both. Severe narrowing is generally a drawing in of all warp ends toward the center rather than of the selvage edges alone, and narrowing of this type caused by excessive warp or weft tension is one of the most dangerous symptoms a weaver's work can show. It frequently causes broken selvage threads and broken ends elsewhere in the fabric. Such a symptom indicates that the weaver must work toward correcting all the weaving skills listed above.

Fastening Weft Ends

New weft threads must be secured inconspicuously but firmly. To fasten a new weft end, throw the shuttle carrying the loose weft and beat the weft into place leaving a short tail of weft at the edge. Without changing the shed carry this weft tail around the edge warp thread and into the shed, under about four top warp threads, and bring it out on top for later

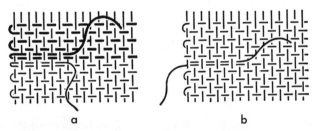

(a) Discontinuing and entering different wefts.
(b) Crossing old and new wefts of the same material.

clipping. A discontinued weft is fastened in the same manner. Insert all new and discontinue all old weft ends in the selvage area, never in the body of the weaving. If the change is merely the starting of a new bobbin of identical material, it is sufficient to cross the old and new weft ends in the new shed under about four warps at the edge.

Cutting the Fabric from the Loom

Before cutting a woven fabric from the loom, loosen the tension on the warp beam and draw the warp forward until the cutting line is about at the breast beam. As soon as the fabric is cut, tie the cut warp in loop knots in groups of two to four inches of warp. This prevents any accident to the warp; and the loop knots are untied when the new tie-in is made by merely pulling the ends.

It is possible to cut the weaving from the loom with little loss of warp and without having to make a new tie-in. After finishing the last fabric, weave about one-half inch of very firm tabby. Insert a wire (a small welding rod is excellent for this purpose) into the shed and weave two more shots to hold it in place. Then cut the fabric at the correct place. The rod can then be lashed to the cloth-beam rod and the weaving resumed with

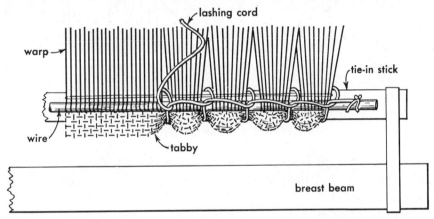

Method for cutting fabric from loom and resecuring it without making new tie-in.

the loss of little more than an inch of warp. The tabby can be "fixed" by painting it with a solution made by squeezing a tube of Duco cement into two ounces of acetone. This fixative, by the way, is very useful for the edges of samples and for other edges which ravel easily.

End Finishes

End finishes for handwoven articles are very important because the finish is part of the over-all craftsmanship of a place mat or a stole and certain other articles. Common finishes are hems and tied or whipped fringes. Where fringes are desired, fold a strip of heavy wrapping paper as wide as the fringe is to be long and weave it into a shed. Or throw four tabby shots unbeaten and beat them down together with short, sharp taps to the position where the new weaving should start, and proceed with the weaving.

The whipping of a fringe can be accomplished most neatly and quickly while the fabric is still stretched on the loom. Thread a needle with a bit of tabby thread. Raise all of the harnesses so that the warp slopes toward the weaver. Start at the right selvage with a tiny knot in the thread. Insert the needle toward the left, under three warp ends and down two tabby ends, and draw it through. Put the needle under the same three warp ends, looping the thread under the needle. Pull the

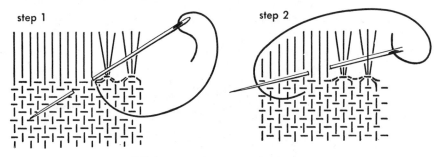

Whipping a fringe on the loom.

thread tight. Then repeat, inserting the needle into the fabric under the next three warp ends and below the second tabby row. This gives a very neat, hemstitched edge. To hemstitch the beginning edge of a fabric, weave about one inch, making the necessary unwoven allowance for the fringe; then work the stitch upside down, but still from right to left.

For pieces which are to be finished with a hem, it is taken for granted that the hems will be made as neat, as strong, and as nearly invisible as possible. To indicate cutting lines for hemmed pieces, throw two tabby shots of a different color and cut between them after the fabric is removed from the loom. Always fold a hem along a single weft and hem it along a single weft.

▶ DRAFTING AND FABRIC ANALYSIS

Drafts and development diagrams are made on cross-section paper. The best type is engineering paper with ten squares per inch and with each full inch square indicated by a heavy line. Equipment for draft-writing and developing includes India ink, a ruling pen and a crow-quill or a fine-line India ink fountain pen, a straight lettering pen with a width of one-tenth of an inch (the Estabrook #13, for instance), and a transparent 45-degree triangle.

Writing Original Drafts

The method of writing original drafts is different for each weave system and requires a technical understanding of the system. In the chapter THE WEAVES AND PATTERN DRAFTS (page 70) an adequate technical analysis of each system taken up is given to enable the weaver to write drafts of his own. Follow the conventions given in the section on The Draft (page 28).

Developing Drafts on Paper

Before threading a pattern on a loom, if a development is not already available, the weaver should always make one. A pattern development is a thread-by-thread, woven-as-drawn-in diagram of the interlacements of a weave, or weaving on paper. To be useful it must include a full draft and a partial repeat in both the warp and the weft directions. Developing on paper helps one understand a weave, and enables one to see in advance exactly what any pattern, orginal or otherwise, will look like. If the pattern is an original one, it helps one to determine whether the arrangement and proportions are right or whether they need altering. It shows how the motifs compose, where the threading should start and end, exactly where motifs start and end (as motifs usually overlap this is particularly important), what element of the pattern will serve as a good border repeat if a border is needed, what the balance figures are, and what the block order and proportions are for making a rose-fashion conversion. The diagram often serves as a great time-saver, since any unhappy thing about a pattern as it adapts to a particular project is revealed in the diagram. There is no risk of wasting time in rethreading or of wasting warp if the development is made in advance.

To make a draft development first set down the draft with a partial repeat at the top of a sheet of cross-section paper. Be sure to draw ink lines at the top and the bottom of the draft so that it is clearly set off and the reading of the harnesses simplified. Draw another horizontal line two or three spaces under the draft to define the top of the development. Draw a perfectly accurate diagonal line starting with the first square of the first space under this line and under the first square or thread symbol of the draft. It is imperative that the diagonal be perfectly accurate, bisecting from corner to corner every square through which it passes. One is now ready to make the development according to the system in which the draft is written.

A Profile Development from a Profile Draft

To make a profile development from a profile draft, in the first (upper) row of the development area put a dot under each square of the first draft block. In most cases this block will be on the A line of the draft. Next, in the same row, place a dot in all the squares which are under squares on the same line of the draft. This is similar to opening a shed for the first block and weaving a shot of black weft through it, and it presupposes a white warp and a white tabby. Next count the number of squares in the first block to determine how many squares down the block must be developed to make it exactly square. Fill in this square block solidly. The diagonal line should emerge from the point—the accuracy check—since

A profile development.

all squares which lie on the diagonal are exactly bisected by the diagonal. Next fill in solid under all the other squares indicated by the dots, for the same number of vertical rows. Each horizontal row indicates a weft shot and all wefts must continue from one edge to the other. It is now time to weave the second block. With an imaginary line trace up from the first square that the diagonal bisects after emerging from the first block, to determine where the second block is and how many squares it contains. "Weave" it as a square on the diagonal line and then "weave" all other blocks on this same line (probably line B) for the same number of spaces. Progress to the third block, and so on until the diagram is a full square. The pattern will be accurate if each square is checked with the diagonal line at the outset.

The diagrams for drafts 77 through 88 are all woven-as-drawn-in developments from profiles. (See pages 134–135.)

A profile development when used for sketching a pattern from a draft for which a profile cannot apply, is called a working profile development (contrasted to a threading profile). Drafts 71 to 76 are illustrated by working profile developments. (See pages 129–132.)

Developments for Twill Drafts

A development for a twill draft requires a predetermined shed sequence. For the basic twill this is 1-2, 2-3, 3-4, 4-1, repeated. Set down several repeats of the draft and draw the diagonal line. As a signal, place the harness numbers 1-2 on the first development line at the right of the draft. Then in the first space of the development fill in every square which lies under threads on harnesses 1 and 2. In the second space write 2-3 at

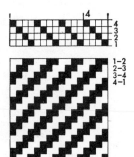

Development of the twill draft.

the right and fill in every square lying under threads on harnesses 2 and 3. In the third space write 3-4 and bring down every thread on harnesses 3 and 4. In the fourth space write 4-1 and bring down every thread on harnesses 4 and 1. Then repeat the whole thing. One peculiarity about the diagonal will be observed. Though each block (two-thread floats are actually called twills) starts where the diagonal emerges from the previous block, just as with the profile development, the diagonal emerges one square in from the corner of the block instead of at the corner. This is a very important point and is a characteristic of all weaving as drawn in with draft systems which are derived from the twill.

Diagrams for fancy twills are not woven as drawn in and therefore the diagonal is not used. At the right of the diagram space set down the shed to be "woven" for each line. Then "weave" it by bringing down the threads indicated for the line. The illustrations on pages 94–95 give fifty-six different four-harness twill patterns which have been diagramed in this manner.

Developments for Overshot Drafts

After setting down one-plus repeats of the draft and drawing the diagonal line underneath, "weave" each block along the diagonal by drawing lines (or filling the squares) under each thread of the draft on the shed being woven. Count the threads in the block which lies above the diagonal at the development point, subtract one, and "weave" that many lines all the way across. There is an important difference here from the profile development. Instead of weaving exact squares along the diagonal, one counts the threads in the block, subtracts one, and "weaves" one shot less than square. The diagonal will emerge one square in from the corner of the block, but at the point where the new block starts. Like the twill, overshot has blocks which share threads with adjacent blocks; there is

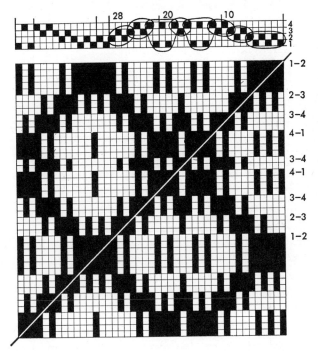

Development for an overshot pattern draft.

always the horizontal overlap of one thread and one must always subtract a single thread to compensate for it vertically.

In the illustrated development above, the first block is on harnesses 1, 2 and has six threads. Therefore fill in, for five lines down, all the squares lying under 1 and 2 threads in the draft. The square just below the lower left corner (the diagonal bisects it) is the "significant square" which indicates the first thread of the next block. This, on the diagram, is a four-thread 2,3 block, so all of the 2's and 3's across the draft are brought down three lines, or shots; this places the significant square under the lower left corner of the block, on harness 3, the first thread of a four-thread 3,4 block. Notice that the next (4,1) is a turning block with five threads and is developed with four shots. All turning blocks have odd numbers of threads and are developed with even numbers of shots, the opposite being true of blocks in straight succession.

Drafts on opposites are developed with actual squares, and the block being developed is brought to the diagonal line at the point. The reason for this is that opposites blocks have no common threads. In drafts which combine opposites and overlapping blocks, the weaver must exercise a certain amount of judgment in deciding from which blocks to subtract a shot, but the diagonal is always there to serve as a guide.

Overshot twill hybrid drafts are developed exactly like overshot drafts.

Developing Crackle Drafts

Crackle drafts are seldom developed in thread-by-thread manner, as the significant thing one needs to learn about them is the block placement. And since few crackle threadings are woven as drawn in, it is the working profile which is generally used. This is illustrated by thread-by-thread developments for drafts 69 and 70 and working profile developments for drafts 71 to 76. (See pages 127–132.)

Developments for Other Draft Systems

Drafts for all weaves in the unit class are developed in profile manner since profiles are used for the threading drafts. Pattern developments for other weaves are either thread-by-thread or from working profiles. Developments are usually avoided in shadow weave and similar systems which depend on color alternations for their pattern, as they tend to become too complicated. They are unnecessary for weaves which depend purely on small interlacements for effect, with the exception of twills.

Textile Analysis

Textile analysis is the process of taking the draft, tie-up, and treadle sequence from a sample of cloth. For known systems in pattern weaves this is simple. One need merely determine the correct block order, count (usually under a textile magnifying glass) the number of threads in each block, and set up the draft according to the rules for the system. The determination of the block order is the important thing. If there is a diagonal line of adjacent blocks, one merely calls the first block A and the second one B. The third one will then be a return to A (one can trace from the block downward to the first line to check this, or to the right, above the first block, to find out if it weaves the same way A weaves), or it will be a new block which one calls C. The fourth block on the diagonal will be either A or B (determined by tracing down or across as before), or it will be a new block called D. When four blocks have been plotted, further blocks are discovered through comparison.

If there is no diagonal development, the problem is a bit different. One searches the sample until a place is found where all four blocks occur in sequence. These four blocks are marked off. (Two rulers, one placed at the top and one at the bottom, are excellent for this purpose.) The four rows of blocks between the rulers are a perfect working profile of the draft. One need only make the assumption of A and B for the first two blocks (a starting point having been determined and a full pattern repeat having been marked off with pins), count the threads under each block in order, and set down the block in its relative position. Some people find this method easier than taking the draft from the diagonal.

Taking the drafts from fancy twills and from fabrics woven in unknown techniques requires considerable knowledge of multiple-harness weaves. This is not a part of the present work.

◀◀
▶ THE WEAVES AND
PATTERN DRAFTS

There are two main groups of weaves, the *controlled weaves* for which the weaver controls the pattern and texture effects by manipulation of warp and weft and the *structural weaves* for which the effects are gained through special harness threadings, harness combinations, and shed sequences. Controlled weaves include brocade, inlay, lace and open-work, tapestry, pick-up, knotted pile, and endless variations within these, most of them produced on two harnesses.

A few widely useful controlled weaves are discussed in the chapter, PLAIN WEAVES, but the structural weaves worked on four harnesses are the main concern of this book. Although weaves and patterns requiring more than four harnesses are not taken up here, it is a mistake to think that four-harness and multiple-harness weaving utilize different technical systems. Most of the multiple-harness weaves are simply extensions of the four-harness weaves; by gaining a true understanding of the four-harness interpretations one has a foundation for understanding the extensions.

The great group of structural weaves is divided into eight classes of systems having similar technical characteristics. The first class is the *plain weave,* all systems under which may be done on two harnesses. Plain weave is also the foundation for many weaves threaded on more harnesses. Next is the simplest of the four-harness threadings, the *twill* class with its many varied systems. Third is the *twill derivative* weaves which expand

70

the overlapping twill combinations to pattern blocks. The *unit class* next has pattern blocks which are individually independent; most of its system structures do not derive directly from the twill. The fifth class is the *grouped thread* weaves in which both warp and weft threads curve together into textured areas. The *double weave* class includes the many textile forms in which two surfaces are woven simultaneously, sometimes in two independent webs, sometimes interlocked, sometimes fully joined. The seventh class embraces the *rhythmic* weaves, a somewhat miscellaneous grouping of various threading systems which are not similar, but each of which is based on a definite threading rhythm. The only class not taken up here is gauze, a truly advanced technique when manipulated by harnesses. *Gauze,* or *leno,* is presented in its controlled weave variation instead.

Each of the classes is subdivided into systems according to the specific threading arrangement, shed composition, and shed sequence which produce the characteristic textures. Thus there are three factors to consider in each weave system: the threading order, the tie-up composition, and the treadling sequence. The most important systems in each class are taken up in detail, while more obscure systems of interest mainly to advanced weavers are omitted.

A further subdivision of the systems lies merely in the different pattern arrangements; so several patterns or threading drafts are given under each system. The basic, classic patterns which, in a general way, are used by all weavers everywhere and have proved themselves through the centuries are included. These are the simple arrangements. In addition other patterns with more elaboration are presented. These are new and previously unpublished as far as can be ascertained and may provide some adventures for the experienced weaver as well as the beginner.

The Classic Weave or Weaving As Drawn In

The handweaver who will understand his weave systems must recognize that for each system there is a basic shedding sequence and warp-weft relationship which gives what is called the classic texture and pattern. In broad generalization the classic interpretation of any weave has balanced structure or background (there are exceptions to this but most of the weaves given here are based on warp-weft balance) and a pattern symmetry which makes the pattern identical whether viewed in the warp-wise or weft-wise direction. The pattern may be a texture pattern produced by variations on thread interlacement, as in the lace and grouped thread weaves, or it may be a pattern formed by floats of a contrasting yarn which pass over and under the base fabric, as in overshot, summer-and-winter, warp pattern and many other systems.

Weaving as drawn in is fundamentally the same for all the weave systems, with differences of detail inherent in each different interlacement sequence. Weaving as drawn in for producing any classic pattern obviates the necessity for written treadling directions. It presupposes that the weaver knows the shed sequence for the system used. After that, one need only weave the pattern blocks systematically as they occur in the developing textile on a 45-degree diagonal line.

Determine by trial and error which pattern treadle weaves the first pattern block at the right-hand edge of the warp, and weave this block until it is square. Then find the treadle which weaves the block lying just to the left of the first block. In a properly tied loom this will generally be the treadle to the right of the first pattern treadle used, though it may be the one to the left. Using this treadle for the pattern, weave the second block until it is square. Then find the treadle which weaves the third block and square the block. These first three blocks will lie corner-to-corner on a hypothetical diagonal line starting at the right-hand selvage and progressing up and to the left at exactly 45 degrees from the horizontal and vertical (warp and weft). It is a good idea to make this hypothetical line tangible by inserting a pin in it and continuing to insert pins as the weaving grows. Continue to select the block which lies exactly to the left of the block just woven, so that the corners touch, and weave the new block until a square is formed. In most balanced weaves the block squaring is accomplished by weaving as many pattern weft shots as there are warp ends involved in the block. For weaves in which blocks overlap (overshot, for instance) a shot must be subtracted to compensate for the overlap. Judgment by eye is the method for squaring blocks in unbalanced weaves, crackle for instance.

The diagonal method is foolproof and is the only reliable method for accomplishing accurate pattern weaving. If the direction of the diagonal wavers or deviates from 45 degrees, blocks are not being squared accurately. If the diagonal breaks, a block or group of blocks has been omitted. If the diagonal jogs, an extra block has been added.

The weaver who trains his eye to see the 45-degree diagonal bisecting the pattern blocks and to select without hesitation the correct block for extending the line is the knowing craftsman who can always weave a pattern correctly, without any previous instructions or written directions, even if the nature of the threading is totally unknown to him. After a little practice, it becomes much easier to weave as drawn in than to follow written treadling directions.

Weaving Pattern and Texture Variations

The classic weave is the foundation for the variations and interpretations of design which are the ultimate aim of most handweavers. There are certain systematic methods for approaching the field of creative weaving and it is usually in the process of systematic experimental investigation, after mastery of the classic form has been attained, that the outstanding new textile designs emerge. Random sampling leads to random designs and effects achieved unwittingly through "happy accidents," though often attractive, have little content or significance. Below are listed the means by which variations of design are achieved.

1. Rearrangement of the treadling sequence to give different patterns.
2. The use with one threading system of the treadling sequence characteristic of other systems.
3. Experiments in color combination and polychrome interpretations (coordinating three or more colors with the pattern or texture sequence to give special color effects).
4. Weaving by special methods for achieving special effects. These are classic methods which differ from weaving as drawn in, and include such weaves as bound, honeycomb, canvas, opposites.
5. The use of non-traditional materials and combinations of materials for warp or weft or both.
6. Combinations of different types and sizes of yarns in studied coordination with the draft or treadling order or both.
7. Unusual spacing of weft or warp or of both.
8. Alteration of the tie-up to produce altogether different textures.

There is a very definite differentiation between the threading system and the weaving method. Failure to understand this leads to considerable confusion, particularly since there are many weaving techniques which are not systems but are weaving methods. If the weaver misses among the systems taken up here such weaves as honeycomb, bound, swivel, canvas, waffle, the reason is that these are methods which are applied to many systems through special handling of the sheds and treadle sequences. They are not weave systems.

▶ THE PLAIN WEAVE
CLASS

The *plain weaves* are those with alternate threads up and down in both warp and weft. They require two harnesses threaded alternately to form two sheds which are woven alternately. Patterns in plain weave are formed through the use of two or more colors or yarn textures in the warp or weft to make stripes, or through crossing a warp stripe with a weft stripe to make plaid. Other pattern types originate from alternating light and dark threads, as in warp and weft rep and log cabin. Plain weaves are produced on any threading which gives the two tabby sheds, and on four-harness looms are more often woven on a twill or some other threading than on the simple, two-harness threading.

Tabby System

Tabby is the most important of all weaves. It has a perfect warp-weft balance and thus employs warp and weft of identical size and fiber type. Strictly speaking, tabby means this balanced plain weave fabric, but common usage has extended the meaning to apply also to the sheds which weave tabby, the treadles which make the sheds, the weft thread for weaving tabby, and the draft arrangement in any system which weaves tabby. These extended meanings of the word are acceptable through common usage, though the word as applied to an unbalanced plain weave fabric is strictly incorrect.

A plaid design in tabby weave.

Unbalanced Plain Weaves

Some plain weaves lack warp-weft balance. These extend all the way from warp set so closely that the weft is completely hidden (warp rep) through all stages of warp emphasis approaching tabby and all stages of weft emphasis to weft rep, which is a complete warp coverage. The reps are heavy fabrics with many interesting applications in rugs, upholsteries, and costume accessories.

Warp rep patterns are formed by alternating two colors in the warp, then threading two ends of one color to create a shift from one block to the next. The illustration on page 76 shows ten different warp-face border patterns with the draft for each one.

Scandinavian people weave warp rep rugs with allover patterns, called Mattor or Matta, by arranging light and dark warp in the manner shown under log cabin but spaced very closely. The patterns are woven by alternating a very heavy weft with a very fine weft to place emphasis on one or the other of the color blocks. Here too block shifts are accomplished through two successive wefts of either the heavy or the fine.

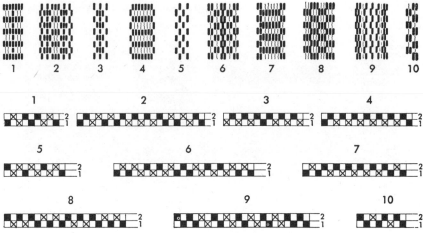

Two harness warp rep patterns.

Weft rep on a widely spaced plain weave warp is made through the use of a soft weft which will beat to cover the warp completely. Patterns and borders are formed through alternating two weft colors and then

Two harness weft rep patterns.

throwing two shots of the same color to accomplish the block shift. Directions for the seven weft rep borders shown in the photograph follow.

First border: light, dark—3 times
                    dark, light—3 times
                    dark
                    dark, light—3 times.

Second border: light, dark—2 times
                    dark, light—5 times
                    dark
                    dark, light—2 times.

Third border: dark, light—2 times
                    light, dark—2 times
                    light—2 times
                    dark—2 times
                    light, dark—2 times
                    light—2 times
                    dark, light—2 times.

Fourth border: light, dark—2 times
                    dark, light—2 times.

Fifth border: dark—2 times
                    light, dark—7 times
                    dark.

Sixth border: dark, light; light, dark
                    light—2 times
                    dark, light; light, dark.

Seventh border: dark—4 times
                    light—2 times
                    dark—2 times; repeat.

Seven further borders are illustrated below. There are infinitely more borders possible in two-color weft rep. By copying these few the learner will gain understanding of the designing system and learn to compose freely.

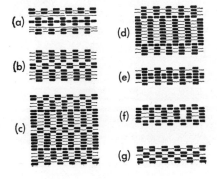

Two harness weft rep patterns.

Basket Weave System

Basket weave is the balanced plain weave in which pairs of threads are alternately up and down. Basket weave has an exact warp-weft balance, and as a consequence the beat requires great control unless the warp sett is unusually close. Three-thread basket uses groups of three threads in

Two-thread and three-thread basket weave.

warp and weft. Commercial monk's cloth is an example of four-thread basket weave.

Spaced Thread System

Warp threads may be grouped by crowding certain reed dents and

Spaced warp, showing a method for weaving spaced weft.

15   14   13

Drafts for spaced warp patterns.

skipping others. Drafts 13, 14, and 15 suggest possible spacing arrangements. Weft may be spaced through beat control or through the use of wires (later removed) in unwoven spaces.

Log Cabin System

A two-block pattern weave on a plain weave threading, usually woven

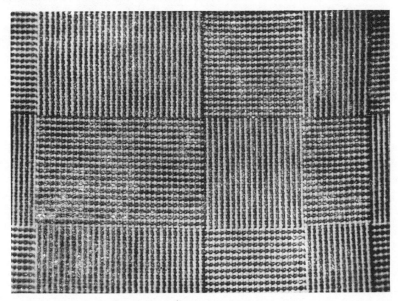

A log cabin design.

as balanced tabby, is descriptively known as *log cabin*. The two-block patterns are formed by the juxtaposition of areas with vertical pin stripes and horizontal pin stripes. The pin stripes are made by alternating dark and light threads in both warp and weft. There are two drafting arrangements possible: repeat sequences with dark on harness 1, light on harness 2; and with light on harness 1, dark on harness 2. The shift from one arrangement (block) to the other is made by placing two threads of the same color together. Thus the shifts may be made on either light or dark

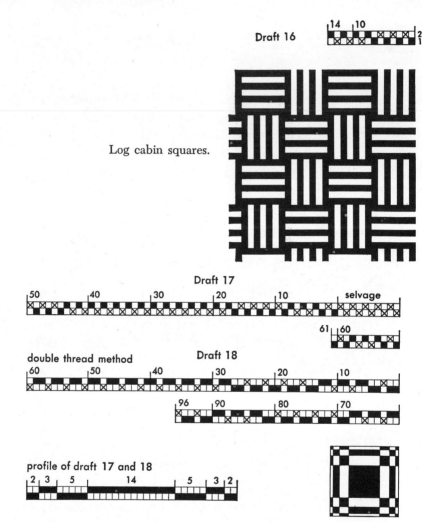

Draft 16

Log cabin squares.

Draft 17

double thread method   Draft 18

profile of draft 17 and 18

A log cabin pattern in two style variations, with its profile.

at the weaver's will. Weft of two colors in alternating shots is used, and pattern block changes are made by throwing two successive shots of either light or dark. Log cabin drafts are generally written in the manner of draft 16, but they may be composed from two-block profiles as shown by drafts 17 and 18.

Log cabin is varied in several ways. A heavy and a fine thread may be alternated, or one of the colors may be doubled to add emphasis as in draft 18. Color stripes may be added. Colors may be alternated in pairs

Draft 19

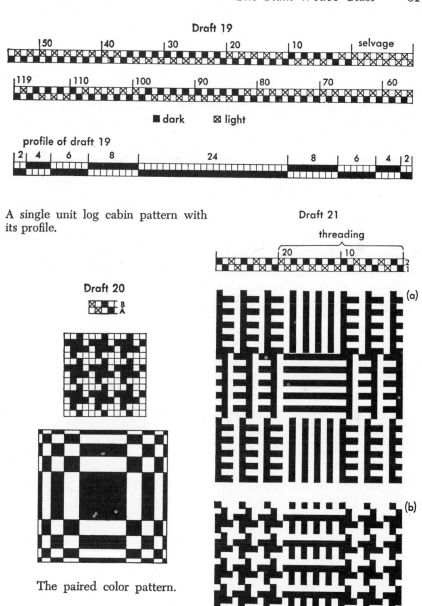

50 40 30 20 10 selvage

119 110 100 90 80 70 60

■ dark ⊠ light

profile of draft 19

2 4 6 8 24 8 6 4 2

A single unit log cabin pattern with its profile.

Draft 21

threading

20 10

(a)

Draft 20

⊠ ■ B
⊠ ■ A

The paired color pattern.

(b)

Combination of light and dark in alternate singles and pairs.

Drafts for pin stripes.

Draft 22   Draft 23

to give tiny spurred checks, as shown in draft 20, and these may be combined with single alternations as in draft 21. Draft 20 is woven: 2 light, 2 dark, repeat. Draft 21(a) is woven: dark, light—5 times; light, dark—5 times. The second figure (b) is 2 dark, 2 light, repeated throughout. Drafts 22 and 23 make narrow stripes by grouping three light or three dark.

◀◀
▶ CONTROLLED
WEAVES ON TABBY
FOUNDATION

Although this book is primarily a study of the structural weaves, a few of the simple controlled weaves are so generally useful and charming that all weavers should know them.

Tabby Inlay

Free patterns, patterns copied from cross-stitch books and other sources, monograms in simple block letters, and original designs transcribed to squared paper may be added to a tabby fabric through *inlay*. Inlays require a fairly open tabby warp and a soft decorating weft thread in addition to a tabby weft, usually like the warp. Short lengths of inlay weft are used, as each separate area of a pattern requires a separate weft. Inlay weft is laid into the tabby shed, as indicated by the diagram and photograph, following each tabby shot or each pair of tabby shots, as desired. The turns from one shed to the next may be made on the surface to strengthen the outline or under the warp by dropping the short pattern weft end through the warp after each row. Loops, as an added decorative detail, may be picked up on a wire or small knitting needle held on top of the warp by inserting the left index finger through the warp at the place a loop is desired and bringing the pattern weft over the

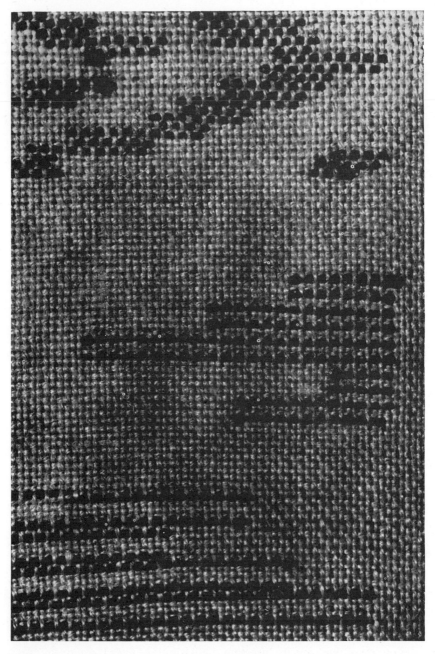

Patterns in simple inlay with turns made on under side. *Top:* inlay in each shed. *Center:* inlay in alternate shed. *Bottom:* paired inlays.

needle. After two or more rows of tabby are woven, the needle is with-drawn for the next row of loops. The diagrams make the methods clear.

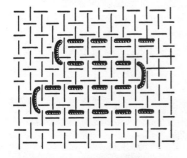

Simple inlay on alternate sheds with turns made on surface.

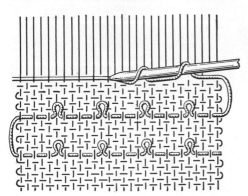
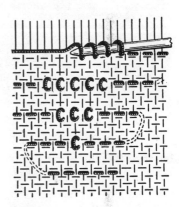

Two styles of inlay loop designs.

Dukagång Inlay

Inlays in the Swedish *Dukagång* manner give a much stronger effect and usually employ a heavier inlay weft. Dukagång is usually done on a twill threading or some other threading by which, through a single tie-up, every fourth thread of the warp is raised to form the inlay shed. It may, however, be woven on two harnesses by picking up on a stick every fourth thread in pattern areas. The inlay weft is dropped through the warp after each row to place turnings on the under side. Weave two tabby shots; open the inlay shed; place the lengths of inlay weft in the desired positions in the shed with the short ends at the left and the long ends at the right, both ends pushed through the warp and dangling underneath; weave two tabby shots; reach through the warp at the place where the second inlay row should start and bring the long end into the shed, carry-

Dukagång with inlay weft following each tabby shot.

ing it to the left as far as the pattern requires, and again drop it through the warp; repeat as required by the pattern. Practice the inlays by making simple squares, oblongs, triangles, and parallelograms until the technique is understood and perfected. Then more elaborate patterns in several colors may be tried. The inlay may be done after each tabby shot if a thicker pattern covering is desired.

Bouquet Lace

Bouquet lace is the simplest of all openwork weaves and is particularly useful because of the speed with which it can be worked and the charming effects it produces. Use a small shuttle which will slip easily in and out of the top warp threads, or a belt shuttle.

1. Weave a foundation of balanced tabby and end with the shuttle at the right, the edge thread up.
2. Open the next tabby shed (edge warp thread down) and keep this shed open while the row of bouquets is worked.
3. Take the shuttle into the shed, under four warp ends, and withdraw it between the fourth and fifth threads.

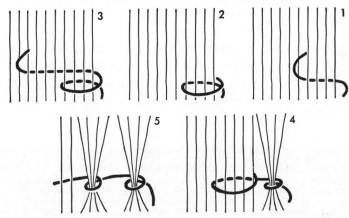

Step-by-step method for weaving bouquet lace. Only top-shed warp threads shown.

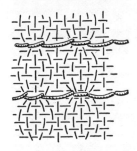

Diagram of classic bouquet lace, encircling three top warp threads.

4. Carry the shuttle back to the right, over these four threads, and insert it into the shed again, carrying it from right to left under eight warp ends, withdrawing it between the eighth and ninth threads.

5. Carry the shuttle back to the right, over four warp ends, and insert it into the shed at the point where it was first withdrawn, and under eight warps.

6. Continue thus across the entire warp, always carrying the shuttle in the shed under eight warp ends, then back on top over four warp ends.

7. Each time a bundle of four top warp ends is encircled, pull the weft so that the threads are drawn tightly together.

8. When the left selvage is reached, beat to place the warps in an even line and as close to the last tabby shot as possible.

9. Weave seven tabby shots; this will bring the shuttle to the right-hand side again, ready for the next row of bouquets.

Bouquets may be woven across only part of the warp distance to form patterns and borders. When this is done it is of even greater importance that the bouquets be beaten so that the openwork row takes up only the space of one tabby shot. Do not be afraid that the effect will be insufficiently open, as the warp and weft threads will rearrange themselves into the groupings when warp tension is released. Work bouquets on a medium-tensioned warp.

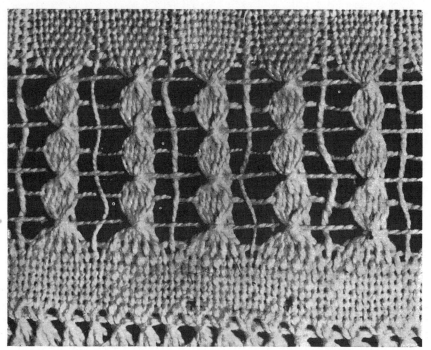

Bouquet lace with only one tabby shot separating bouquets.

Pick-up Leno

Leno is particularly useful for making beautiful, hemstitched-like finishes and for lacy borders. The weave requires the use of a pointed hardwood pick-up stick which is longer than the width of the warp. Many variations are possible, including the working of all leno fabrics. Two-around-two leno in successive rows is especially effective if pairs are split on alternate pick-up rows to form diagonal lines. Combinations of two or more leno styles are an ancient technique as in Tarascan lace, with patterns formed of one-around-two leno on a background of two-around-two.

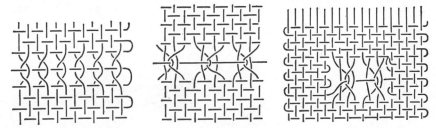

Three styles of pick-up leno: single leno, two-around-two leno, and leno with built-up tabby areas.

Leno variations. Top to bottom: one-around-two, three-around-three, two-around-two, and one-around-one leno.

If leno is combined with tabby areas to form patterns, the tabby areas must be built up on both sides of leno.

1. Weave a tabby heading and end with the shuttle at the right and the edge thread down.
2. Change sheds and hold the shed open while making the pick-up.
3. With the index finger pick up the first thread of the bottom warp (second thread of the total warp) and bring it to the right and up around the first thread of the top warp on the pick-up stick.
4. With the pick-up stick (or finger) reach between the first and second threads of the top warp and pick up the second thread of the bottom warp; pull it to the right and up on the stick.
5. Continue thus across the warp until every thread of the bottom warp is held on the stick above the top warp, exchanging the positions of top and bottom warp.
6. Release the treadle; turn the pick-up stick on edge, push it against the reed, and run the shuttle through the narrow shed.
7. Treadle the next shed. Beat very sharply so that the twists are forced as tightly as possible against the tabby. Throw weft through this shed and beat as tightly as possible. In correctly woven leno, the twist requires the same amount of space as one weft shot.
8. Repeat the leno pick-up if desired, or continue with tabby weaving.

Leno has many variations; a simple one which makes a lacier effect is the two-thread leno. This is worked in the manner described above except that two threads are picked up together from the bottom shed and carried to the right around two top warp threads, and the second pick-up is made between the second and third top warp threads. Pick-ups are continued in pairs across the warp. This is a larger twist which should require about the space of two tabby shots.

The effectiveness of leno depends on the firmness of the weave. Therefore the weft must be beaten sufficiently to prevent the edge tabby shots from moving toward the twist when warp tension is released. Contrary to the inexperienced weaver's usual concept, sleazy leno is not as open and lacy as firm leno.

◀◀ ▶ THE TWILL CLASS

Twill is the simplest of all threadings for more than two harnesses. The basic twill employs the harnesses in regular succession repeated continuously. Although twill may be threaded on three harnesses (an example is the common jeans or Genoa twill) and also may be extended to as many harnesses as the weaver wishes to employ, its widest use is in the four-harness interpretation. And the use is very wide indeed, as twill ranks next to tabby in importance.

The *circle diagram* is a means for understanding the twill and all weaves derived from it. A circle is bisected horizontally and vertically and the harnesses are represented by the points where the four spokes touch the circle's periphery. Harnesses are numbered clockwise in the twill draft order: 1, 2, 3, 4. The continuous circuit of the diagram represents the twill threading and shows the actual relationships of harnesses, with the interval from 4 to 1 identical with the other three intervals. The harnesses alternate odd-even, even-odd, regardless of the starting point or the direction of movement around the circle. The functioning twill, through its tie-up, uses pairs of adjacent harnesses. These pairs necessarily combine an odd- and an even-numbered harness:

the A combination is 1-2, the B combination is 2-3,
the C combination is 3-4, the D combination is 4-1.

91

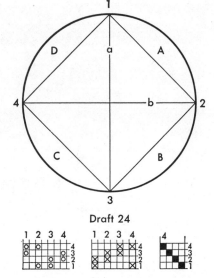

The circle diagram from which the twill draft, twill tie-up and treadling order are composed.

Draft 24

Each harness of a combination is shared with the two adjacent combinations. Thus the sequences always overlap as one progresses around the circle. Two further harness combinations are possible, those which join the odd-numbered harnesses and those which join the even-numbered ones; these defy the twill and form tabby sheds, a characteristic of all threadings related to twill.

Basic Twill System

Basic twill as described above is drafted 1, 2, 3, 4, repeated continuously. Fundamentally it is a balanced weave and thus it is usually used. However, it may be interpreted, like the plain weave, in the full range of warp emphasis and weft emphasis. The twill selvage is a tabby threading of two odd-numbered threads followed by two even-numbered threads: 1, 3, 2, 4. This selvage threading is employed however only if the weaving is to be done in the regular 1-2, 2-3, 3-4, 4-1 order.

Many variations of the balanced twill known as *fancy twills* are made through the use of a light-colored warp and dark weft, or vice versa, woven with unconventional sheds and shed orders. The balanced (two-up-two-down) combinations of the circle diagram give, as has been pointed

Twill stripes and tabby plaids on the same warp.

out, six different sheds. There are, however, eight further sheds of an unbalanced nature which may be used. These are made by raising a single harness: 1, 2, 3, 4; or by raising three harnesses together: 1-2-3, 2-3-4, 3-4-1, 4-1-2. Thus there are actually fourteen possible twill sheds, and these fourteen sheds can be utilized in different groupings and orders to form almost limitless patterns. Illustrated on pages 94–95 are fifty-six four-harness twill patterns in diagram, and there are many more which the weaver can discover at the loom. The threading for all of these is 1, 2, 3, 4, repeated. The tie-up, or shed composition, and the shed order for each are shown by the figures at the right of each diagram. These diagrams presuppose a white warp and a black weft.

The Color Effect Twills

Another traditional method for introducing interesting pattern and stripe effects into the twills is by the use of two or more colors in both warp and weft. The color effects are most striking when the values of the two colors are in strong contrast; the strongest combination is of course

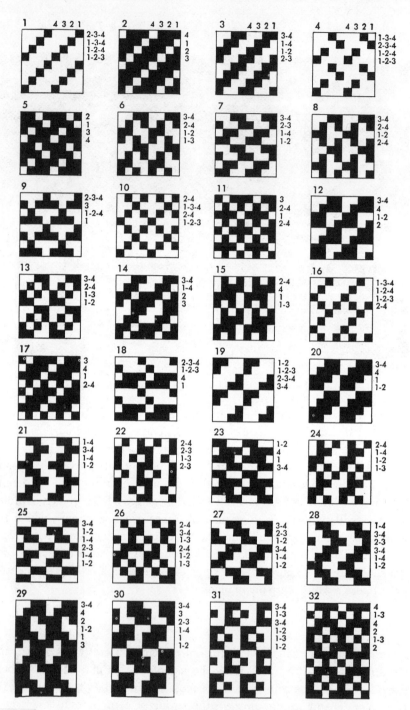

Diagrams for straight and fancy twills.

94

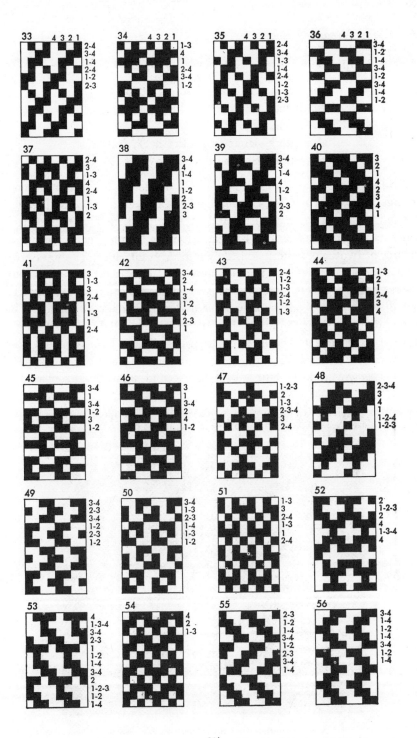

33   4 3 2 1
2-4
3-4
1-4
2-4
1-2
2-3

34   4 3 2 1
1-3
4
1
2-4
3-4
1-2

35   4 3 2 1
2-4
3-4
1-3
1-4
2-4
1-2
1-3
2-3

36   4 3 2 1
3-4
1-2
1-4
3-4
1-2
3-4
1-4
1-2

37
2-4
3
1-3
4
2-4
1
1-3
2

38
3-4
4
1-4
1
1-2
2
2-3
3

39
3-4
3
1-4
4
1-2
1
2-3
2

40
3
2
1
4
2
3
4
1

41
3
1-3
3
2-4
1
1-3
1
2-4

42
3-4
2
1-4
3
1-2
4
2-3
1

43
2-4
1-2
1-3
2-4
1-2
1-3

44
1-3
2
1
2-4
3
4

45
3-4
1
3-4
1-2
3
1-2

46
3
1
3-4
2
4
1-2

47
1-2-3
2
1-3
2-3-4
3
2-4

48
2-3-4
3
4
1
1-2-4
1-2-3

49
3-4
2-3
3-4
1-2
2-3
1-2

50
3-4
1-3
2-3
1-4
1-3
1-2

51
1-3
3
2-4
1-3
1
2-4

52
2
1-2-3
2
4
1-3-4
4

53
4
1-3-4
3-4
2-3
1
1-2
1-4
3-4
2
1-2-3
1-2
1-4

54
4
2
1-3

55
2-3
1-2
1-4
3-4
1-2
2-3
3-4
1-4

56
3-4
1-4
1-2
1-4
3-4
1-2
1-4

95

black and white. The colors are alternated in different ways:

1 light, 1 dark—Stairstep Twill, draft 25
2 light, 2 dark
3 light, 3 dark
4 light, 4 dark—Hound's Tooth Check, draft 27
6 light, 6 dark—Shepherd's Check, draft 28

Several of these have traditional names as indicated. Further traditional arrangements are the Glen Urquhart which alternates sections threaded 2, 2 and 4, 4 as shown in drafts 30 and 32. Another is the Gun Club Check which is two repeats of the 4-thread Hound's Tooth Check with dark squares of two colors alternated, shown in draft 29. Draft 31 shows a 2,2 color alternation used in a manner similar to log cabin. This gives very diverse pattern effects when woven with different color sequences. The first diagram shows one shot of light and one of dark alternated. The second diagram shows 2 dark, 2 light twice; 2 dark; 1 light; 2 dark, 2 light twice; 1 dark; repeat. The third diagram is 4 dark, 4 light repeated. The diagrams under draft 32 show similar variations on a 2,2 and 4,4 draft. The first is woven dark, light, repeat; the second, light, dark, repeat. The

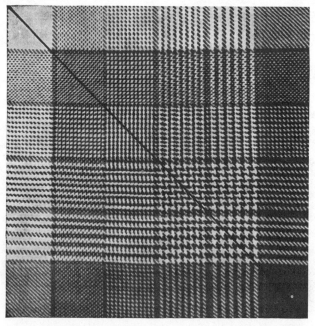

A twill color-effect gamp or sample range.

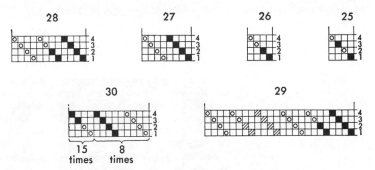

Drafts for color effect twills.

Draft 31

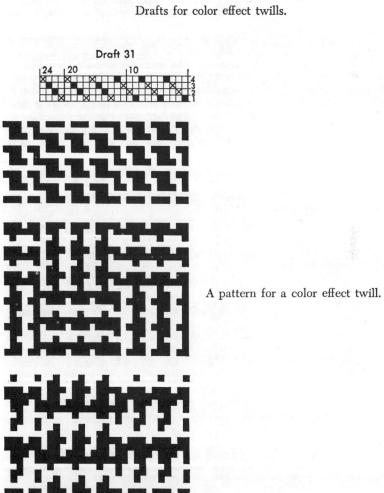

A pattern for a color effect twill.

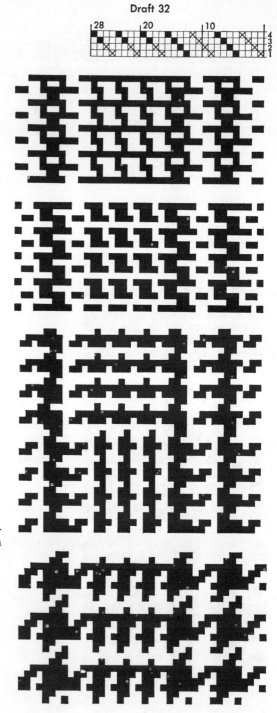

A Glen Urquhart type two-color twill threading with pattern variations.

third is 2 dark, 2 light four times; 1 light, 2 dark, 1 light 4 times; repeat. The fourth diagram is 4 dark, 4 light; repeat. Weaving is always in twill order.

The photograph on page 96 is a so-called "gamp" or sample in which equal sections are threaded in various arrangements and then woven as drawn in to show the typical patterns along the 45-degree diagonal and the variations in the other squares. The threading is (1) all black; (2) 4 black, 4 white; (3) 3 black, 3 white; (4) 2 black, 2 white; (5) 1 black, 1 white; (6) all white. The treadling is always in standard twill order.

The Point Twill System

If a "return" is made at the end of a twill threading, the result is a *point twill,* which reads 1, 2, 3, 4, 3, 2, repeat. This is the simple point twill often known as bird's-eye. The forward or backward progression may be longer than four threads as plotted on the circle diagram, but it must be at least

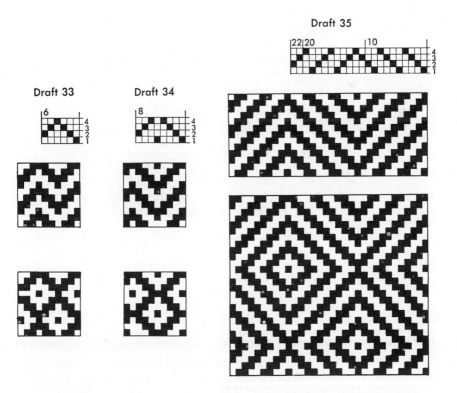

Point Twills: Draft 33, birds-eye; draft 34, rosepath; draft 35, goose-eye.

three threads (harnesses). Aside from the direction reverse, the point twill differs from the basic twill in that it has floats of three-thread and one-thread length at each point when woven with the balanced tie-up.

The six-thread, the eight-thread and a longer point twill are shown on drafts 33, 34 and 35, for comparison. Two developments are shown for the point twills, one "woven" in twill order, the other with shed order duplicating the draft order. The eight-thread point twill is one of the most used of drafts and is known as rosepath, or rosengang by the Swedish. When there are ten or more threads forward with a symmetrical return, the pattern is known as goose-eye, draft 35.

The illustration below shows how one of the fancy twill treadlings may be used with point twill threadings to give patterns of considerable elaboration.

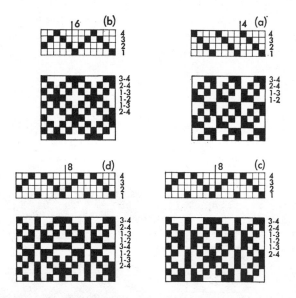

A fancy twill with draft and pattern extensions from it.

The Extended Point Twill System

Twills with more than two returns, drafted in symmetrical or asymmetrical fashion, are known as *extended point twills*. Extended point twills form patterns of varying intricacy and are useful where a patterned surface with close-woven texture in a single weft is desired. One of the very useful threadings is chromatic textures, draft 36, so named because

Draft 36

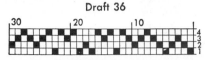

Chromatic textures.

Stripes in chromatic textures threading. Singles linen warp and weft.

it provides a solution for the very difficult problem of producing effective multi-color borders in single-shuttle linen and wool weaving. Chromatic textures is a classic progression of three-harness point twills, the first starting on harness 1, the second on harness 2, the third on 3 and the fourth on 4, with a return. Draft 37, Chinook, is one of countless similar patterns, which are usually woven as drawn in, often with a tabby in the overshot manner.

Rules for extended point twills are the same as for point twill, but they allow more freedom because a single pattern repeat has more than two points and the arrangement need not be symmetrical.

Draft 37

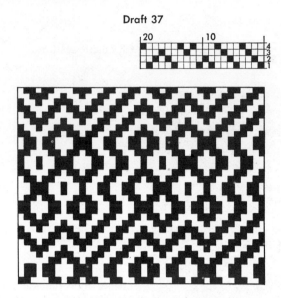

Chinook, an extended point twill pattern.

Broken Twill System

Because the three-thread floats of the point will create a disfigurement and also a weakness in the twill-woven fabric, weavers in ages past devised a method for eliminating the break, and thus strengthening the fabric and creating clear-cut lines. This was done by simply omitting one thread of the point combination, a trick which required that the balance of the point twill be retained through number rather than through symmetry. Thus, the point twill changes from 1,2,3,4,3,2, repeat, to 1,2,3,4,2,-1,4,3, repeat. The 3,4,3 and the 2,1,2 of the original draft have become simply 3,4 and 1,2, and a break in the twill succession occurs, giving the name, *broken twill*.

The broken twills form an exception to the circle diagram rule of odds and evens. As a consequence, these threadings will not weave a tabby. The broken twills, or dorniks as they are often called, are used in the weaving of wool yardages and for producing special effects.

The photograph shows at the right the rosepath draft, in the second square a simple extended point twill, in the third the broken goose-eye, in the fourth the four-thread broken twill and at the left the crowfoot or two-thread broken twill. The weaving is in standard twill sequence.

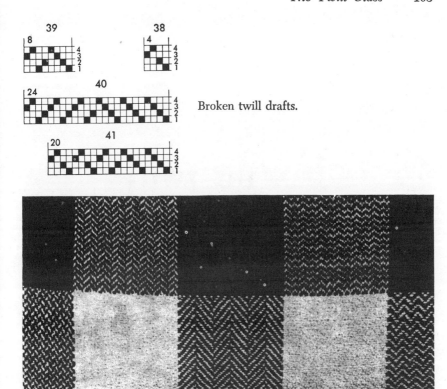

Broken twill drafts.

Twill variations woven as straight twills. Left to right: Draft 38; draft 39; draft 40; an extended point twill threaded 1,2,3,4,3,2,1,2,3,2, repeat; draft 34.

◄◄
▶ THE TWILL
DERIVATIVE CLASS

Twill derivative weaves are derived directly from the twill and follow all the rules of the twill class. The threadings and treadlings may be plotted on the circle diagram; all progressions are from odd to even or from even to odd; the standard balanced tie-up is used for weaving in the classic manner. The exception of jumping from an odd to an odd or from an even to an even which occurs in the broken twills is never used in the drafting of twill derivative weaves, but it does occur in certain weaving methods and is known as "weaving on opposites." This means jumping from a 1-2 combination to the opposite 3-4 combination, or from 2-3 to 4-1, and so on. The classic method for weaving each of the twill derivatives differs according to the draft type, even though the tie-up is that used for twill, and treadling progressions follow the circle diagram. Selvages for all weaves derived from twill are the twill succession.

The Overshot System

Of all the weaves for simple or elaborate patterns, *overshot* is the best known, the most used, and therefore the most important. It is popular because it can easily be adapted through both drafting and treadling sequence to the widest imaginable variety of patterns and textures, and because it is so perfectly expressed in four-harness threadings with the

104

balanced tie-up. In America the traditional use of the weave for the classic colonial coverlet gives to it much special interest and renown, but the system has been widely used elsewhere throughout the world during many centuries.

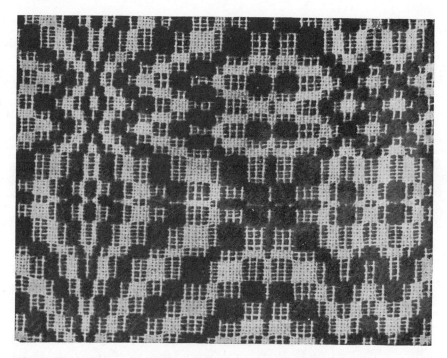

Classically woven-as-drawn-in overshot showing the pattern blocks in weft floats, the background areas in balanced tabby and half-tones separating the two.

The new weaver who troubles to study drafts is always amazed at the realization of the simple manner in which the overshot draft system develops from the point twill draft, and the weaver who does understand this is immediately equipped to draft his own patterns and to take the draft from any fabric or photograph of one woven in overshot. The secret of the whole matter lies in the odd-even progressions and the odd-even combinations.

The draft at the top of page 106 is the twill draft (with the first thread of the repeat added) and the four twill (odd-even) combinations circled. Next, each one of the combinations is enlarged by repeating the pair of threads once before passing on to the next combination. The result is the twelve-thread draft of the twill succession of blocks, each block of mini-

Draft 42

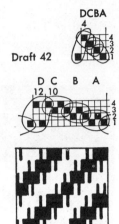

Overshot blocks arranged in twill (A,B,C,D, repeat) order.

mum four-thread size. Each or any combination might have been repeated more times to form blocks of six, eight, ten or more threads. Note that every block has an even number of threads, and each shares a thread on both sides with its neighboring block, making one-thread overlaps. When any one of these blocks is woven, the weft will float over the four threads of the block, or "shoot" over it; hence the name overshot. The diagram under the twill succession draft shows exactly how the pattern weft threads compose, supposing that one is using a white warp and tabby and a black pattern weft. Notice that there are three distinct areas: solid black or pattern weft blocks, solid white or tabby background areas, and intermediate areas in which pattern weft passes over alternate warp threads to form half-tones. Larger blocks would have more half-tone lines above and below them. As may be observed, there is a half-tone to the right and to the left and also at the bottom and the top of each block. Each block overlaps its adjacent blocks by the width of one warp thread. These are the fundamental characteristics of the overshot technique.

One further overshot characteristic shows up only when the combination enlargement system is applied to the point twill. The "rosepath" point twill is at the top of page 107 and below it the four-block diamond which results when it is enlarged. Notice that the turning, or return, blocks contain five threads, the additional thread being the one which changes the draft direction. The diagrams are made as normal woven-as-drawn-in developments along a diagonal. Exact squares are not woven, but the blocks are under-squared by one line to compensate for the overlap. Observe that

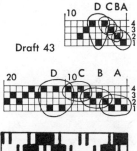

The four-block overshot diamond, derived from the point twill.

in drafting, blocks in straight progression have an even number of threads and turning blocks have an odd number of threads, while in weaving this convention is reversed.

The minimum size for an overshot block is set by the twill combination plus a single repeat and is therefore four threads. Turning blocks have the combination repeated and the return thread added, so that the minimum block would normally be five threads. However, it is common practice to use the three-thread return block if this enhances the character of the pattern. The size of the block is determined by the number of times the twill combination is repeated, and this in turn is determined by the practical length for a weft float. This limitation must be considered since blocks are formed of full length weft floats; the density of the warp sett helps determine what is practical: a ten-thread float would be only one-quarter of an inch long at forty ends per inch, but would be two-thirds of an inch at fifteen per inch.

Overshot is a two-shuttle weave with a tabby foundation. A tabby shot of weft identical to the warp precedes each shot of pattern weft and tabbies alternate. The beat must be sharp to place the tabby at exactly as many shots per inch as there are warp ends and to force the pattern weft into the minute spaces between tabby shots. Because of this crowding, a light weight woolen or worsted yarn is good material for pattern weft, and soft strand cottons and mercerized floss can be used. The Swedish weavers have a special interpretation of overshot in all linen using a fine singles as pattern weft. If the pattern weft is to be heavy or inflexible it is necessary to space the warp more widely than one normally would.

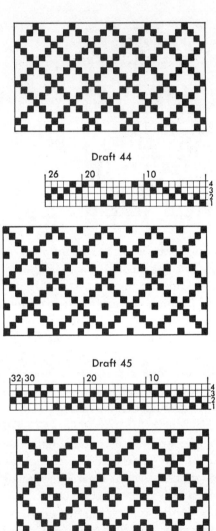

Draft 44

Overshot diamonds illustrated by working profiles: four-block diamond, draft 43; five-block diamond, draft 44; six-block diamond, draft 45.

Draft 45

Above is a reduced working profile development of the four-block diamond with several repeats, and similar diagrams for the five-block (draft 44) and the six-block (draft 45) diamond. The five-block diamond develops from a point twill with six forward moving threads, the six-block diamond from a point twill with seven forward moving threads. The diamond motifs are the foundation for all overshot pattern drafting.

The second motif is the "table" formed by pausing at the return point of a diamond and drafting back and forth for seven or more blocks. Draft 46 shows this table on blocks D and A, all blocks of minimum size. Draft

Draft 46

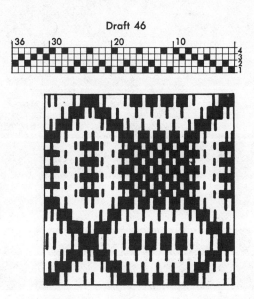

Diamond and table, two simple overshot motifs combined.

46 also shows the third overshot motif, the cross, a five-block return arrangement appearing here as C-B-A-B-C.

Draft 47 (page 110) is similar to 46 but each diamond is centered with a star instead of a table. The photograph shows part of a sampler with pattern borders which are variations instead of woven-as-drawn-in developments.

The star motif is a five-block alternation between two draft blocks in which the center block is smaller than the two on each side of it. Draft 48 (page 111) shows two stars drafted together to form a complete pattern. The first star is blocks A,B,A,B,A; the second one, blocks D,C,D,C,D. Stars have the significant characteristic of becoming roses if the woven blocks are inverted while star proportions are retained. The second diagram shows the same draft woven as roses by using the treadles in B,A,B,A,B and C,D,C,D,C order instead of in the drafted order, but retaining the exact proportions (number of shots per block) of the star develop-

Borders woven on star and diamond threading.

Star and diamond (or cross).

Draft 47

ment. Rose-fashion is actually another method of weaving as drawn in, but it is a rather tricky method which usually requires the working out of the weaving directions in advance and treadling from them. First work out the woven-as-drawn-in directions for star-fashion development on paper, and determine through examination of the development which pair of blocks will form the main rose figure. Then set up a conversion table for switching the block order. The conversions must be complete, meaning that the two blocks not involved in the main star figure must also be reversed in the weaving. If the main star is on A,B or C,D,

Block B is woven where A occurs in the star,
Block A is woven where B occurs in the star,
Block D is woven where C occurs in the star,
Block C is woven where D occurs in the star.

If the main star is on B,C or D,A,

Block A is woven where D occurs in the star,
Block D is woven where A occurs in the star,
Block C is woven where B occurs in the star,
Block B is woven where C occurs in the star.

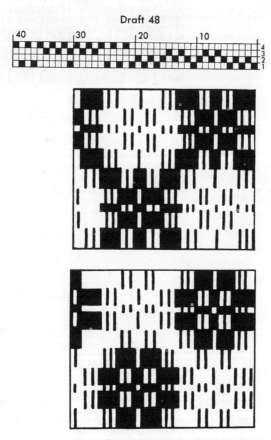

Draft 48

Staggered stars developed as stars and roses.

Draft 49

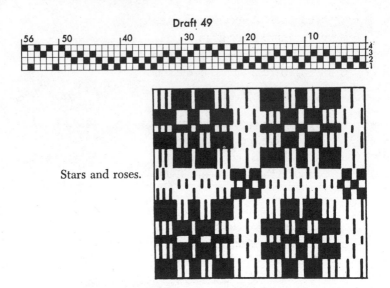

Stars and roses.

Draft 49 which weaves roses and stars simultaneously will help illustrate the rose-fashion system. In this case the two figures are drafted, so that the roses weave without any conversions being made. Notice that one motif is drafted A,B,A,B,A and the other one B,A,B,A,B. A transition figure is added to separate the star from the rose, of necessity an asymmetrical figure that adds a slight irregularity to the pattern.

Christmas Star or Christmas Rose, as draft 50 is called, is an elaborated diamond and star with emphasis achieved through the use of blocks of different sizes. The rose-fashion diagram given below shows how diamonds often recompose to form the wheel motif when this weaving method is employed. Draft 51 (page 114), Hot Springs, shows another variation of diamond with table and cross, a small pattern which weaves very handsomely. Further draft variation with emphasis provided by one large block forms the elaborate flower figure of draft 52 (page 115) called Morning Glory. This pattern is delicately beautiful and yet strong.

A further motif is the multiflora. Multiflora is two flower motifs of minimum size used alternately; it is so simple that it is subject to a wide range of technical variations and is one of the most versatile of drafts. Draft 53 (page 116) is the basic multifloral. The perceptive weaver will recognize this draft as a variation of the five-block diamond, strengthened through the use of large and small blocks.

Draft 50

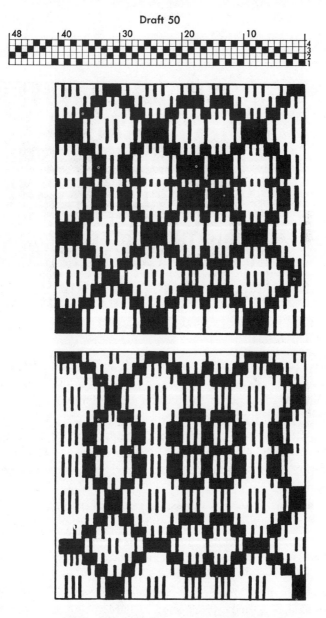

Christmas Star with both star-fashion and rose-fashion developments.

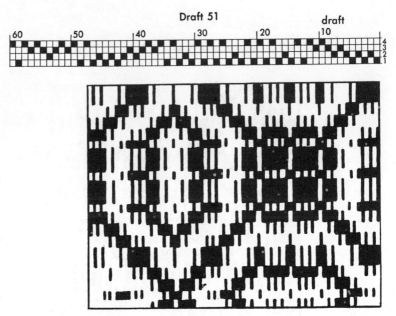

Hot Springs.

Overshot Opposites

Because the *opposites* differ in both draft and treadling from the fundamental overshot system, they are best understood if taken up as a separate system, though some prefer to consider them simply a variation of overshot.

The opposites principle is easily understood. Opposites are compensating pairs: 1,2 and 3,4 are opposites whether drafted as blocks, connected as tie-ups or woven as sequences. Likewise 2,3 and 4,1 are opposites, and also 1,3 and 2,4.

There are two types of opposites overshot patterns, two-block and four-block. An example of the two-block is the historic Monk's Belt pattern which is simply a single star drafted on opposites, followed by alternating two-thread "blocks." As seen in draft 54 (page 117), the star is drafted on A,C,A,C,A. Blocks B and D are not included. A study of the diagram, which gives Monk's Belt border arrangements (star-fashion at the top, rose-fashion at the bottom), shows what happens when the intermediate blocks are eliminated: all half-tones are eliminated. The pattern is strong and clear-cut, unblurred by the half-tone value. Patterns for two-block opposites may be drafted from two-block profiles through substituting 1,2 for A and 3,4 for B, but the longest block of a profile can be no longer than the maximum feasible float length.

Draft 52

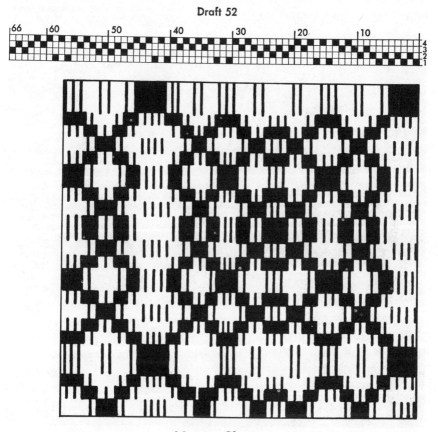

Morning Glory.

Four-block opposites add a complexity and a resulting distortion to the opposites weave. The theory is that intermediate blocks omitted from an opposites draft may be employed in a separate position as another set of opposites. Draft 55 (page 118) illustrates this principle. It shows also that the half-tones, missing in the two-block opposites, return when the two intermediate blocks are added, but in unconventional positions. The advantage of drafts of this type is that they have more strength and more sparkle than ordinary overshot because the main black and white areas are adjacent.

Observe the development for the opposites drafts 56, 57, and 59 (pages 118–120). Within the half-tone areas occur two-thread twill floats and two-thread tabby. These are called accidentals, as they are unavoidable technical irregularities resulting from the forcing of the draft. They can be controlled through careful drafting, but cannot be eliminated.

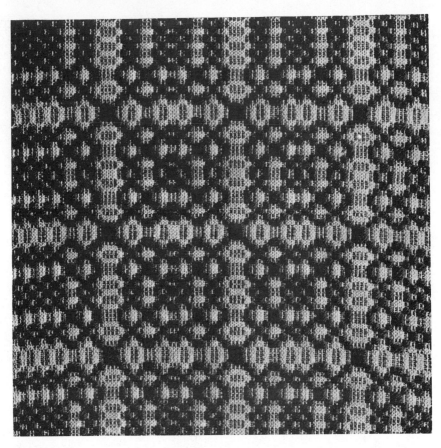

Morning Glory with border made by repeating threads 18 to 27. Warp and tabby of 20/2 cotton at 30 ends per inch, pattern weft of 2/18 worsted.

Draft 53

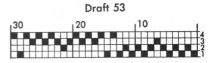

Multiflora.

Draft 54

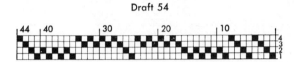

Monk's Belt, a classic **opposites** pattern. A few Monk's Belt borders showing stars at top, roses at bottom.

Draft 56 (page 118) shows two opposites stars drafted with even-number blocks (though there is a transitional irregularity here too). Draft 57 (page 119) is two stars drafted with an odd number of threads in each block, a technique which obviates the irregularity and also organizes the accidentals better than when blocks have an even number of threads.

Draft 58 (page 120) shows the little multiflora drafted on opposites; it has been possible to eliminate the transition block used in draft 53. The first development shows it woven in the conventional manner as opposite flowers but with overlapping centers. The second development interprets it as a true two-block opposites pattern by weaving the centers as one-thread 1,2 and 3,4 blocks. Draft 59 (page 120) is another symmetrical opposites multiflora with the two figures placed on adjacent rather than opposite

Draft 55

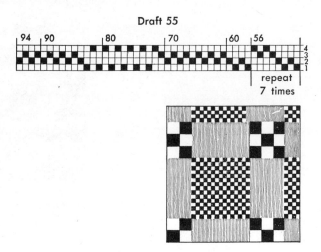

A "patchwork" opposites pattern.

Draft 56

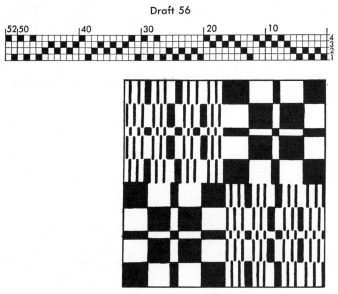

Opposite stars, a redrafting of draft 48 to shift the half-tones away from the pattern blocks. Illustrates occurrence of accidentals along with half-tones.

blocks to introduce the softening effect of half-tones. The first diagram shows a true opposites development while the second diagram shows a softened interpretation made by weaving the transition twill in strict overshot manner.

Draft 57

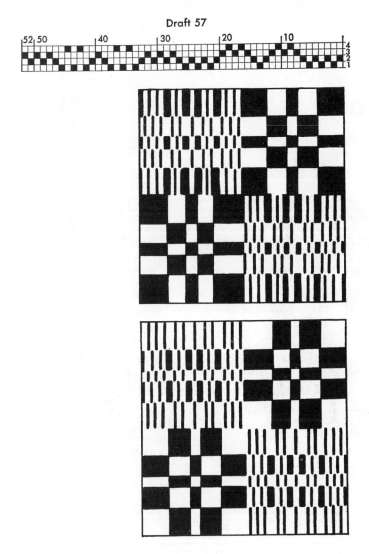

Symmetrical draft for opposite stars. Developed also as roses.

Occasionally drafts will combine normal overshot motifs with opposites motifs, as illustrated by Moon Wake, draft 60 (page 120). For such a threading it occasionally happens that the design will be handsomer if the entire pattern is woven in normal overshot manner and the transition intervals are woven as twills.

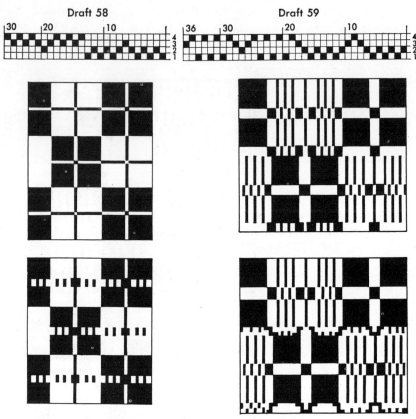

Opposites multiflora drafts. The diagrams illustrate the two methods for interpreting small woven-as-drawn-in-overshot opposites.

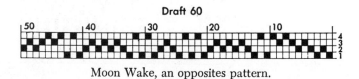

Moon Wake, an opposites pattern.

The Overshot-Twill Hybrid System

Drafts combining twill successions with overshot blocks might be looked upon as overshot (and too often erroneously are) were it not for a technical peculiarity. The twills interweave very closely, whereas overshot blocks interweave relatively openly. Therefore the weaving of threadings in which blocks are interspersed with twills requires a somewhat wider warp sett, a relatively finer warp thread, or a much stronger beat than overshot threadings. Another difference is that these threadings, because of the intimate relationship between tabby and pattern weft, require a much closer attention to the rule that blocks in straight succession are woven with an odd number of shots and turning blocks with an even number of shots. Failure to obey this rule when weaving hybrid threadings results in the disfigurement of the pattern beyond recovery, whereas

Draft 61

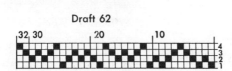

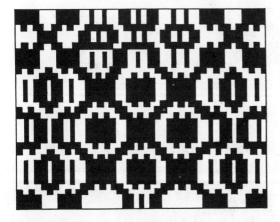

Primrose, a hybrid (overshot-twill) pattern.

Draft 62

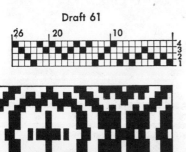

Dewy Web, a hybrid pattern.

with overshot threadings there is no disfigurement, merely the possibility of a slightly unsymmetrical pattern.

Draft 63

China Doll, hybrid (overshottwill).

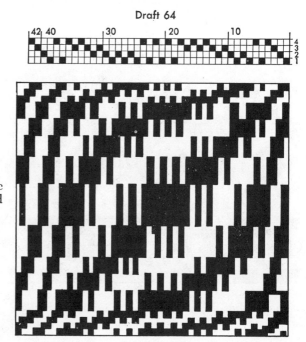

Draft 64

Magnolia, the classic leaf motif in hybrid (overshot-twill).

Draft 65

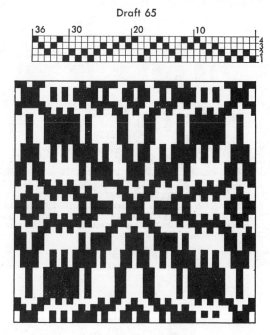

Oriole, hybrid (overshot-twill).

Draft 66

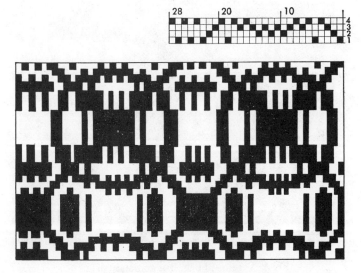

Candlelight, hybrid (overshot-twill).

Contour, hybrid (overshot-twill).

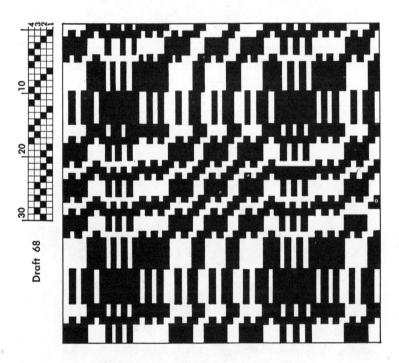

Shish Kebab, hybrid (overshot-twill).

Hybrid patterns are popular for weaving borders on articles such as towels, mats, and scarves, and for making small calico-like allover patterns. The asymmetrical arrangements are particularly attractive.

The Crackle System

Crackle is a weave derived from the point twill in an altogether different manner from overshot. The repeat unit for each of the four crackle blocks is a three-harness point twill. The circle diagram makes the arrangement and association of each of these blocks plain. Block A is the three-harness point twill starting on harness 1; therefore it is 1,2,3,2; block B is 2,3,4,3; block C, 3,4,1,4; block D, 4,1,2,1. Any of these units may be drafted alone, or may be repeated at will to compose blocks of any desired

The four crackle units with their transition threads.

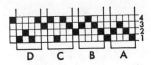

size. However, since each block ends with the starting thread of the next block, it is necessary to add a transition thread at the end of a block, and this is placed on the same harness as the first thread of the unit. Thus, the transition thread ending block A is on harness 1, that for block B on harness 2, for block C on 3, for block D on 4. The diagram above is simply the diagram of these units with the transition thread for each, but it may be used as a draft by repeating each unit as desired.

Crackle may be woven with tabby and pattern shots alternating, like overshot. However the classic crackle method omits the tabby and follows the rhythm of the draft with the use of three shuttles, each carrying a different color of thread. Treadle in the following sequences using the standard tie-up:

Block A—treadle 4, first background color,
        "   1, main color,
        "   2, second background color,
        "   1, main color,
  end with   "   4, first background color, for the transition.

Block B—treadle 1, first background color,
        "   2, main color,
        "   3, second background color,
        "   2, main color,
  end with   "   1, first background color, for the transition.

Block C—treadle 2, first background color,
         "   3, main color,
         "   4, second background color,
         "   3, main color,
end with "   2, first background color, for the transition.

Block D—treadle 3, first background color,
         "   4, main color,
         "   1, second background color,
         "   4, main color,
end with "   3, first background color, for the transition.

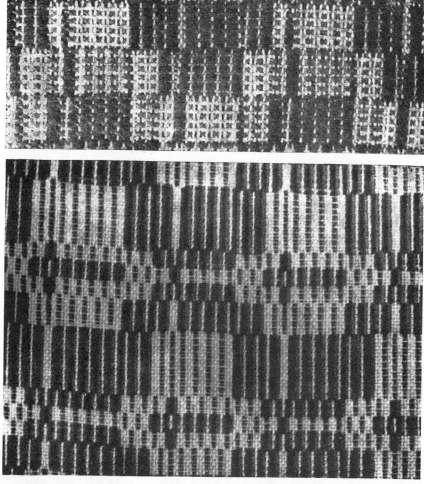

Crackle woven in classic manner (above) and in overshot method (below).

The photograph shows a crackle threading woven both in the overshot manner and in the classic no-tabby crackle manner with a heavy dark and two fine light colors. The draft for this is an irregular diamond as follows: A once, B once, C twice, D five times, A once, D twice, C twice, B five times, repeat.

Weaving as drawn in is not commonly attempted in crackle, though the Swedish books contain many crackle (called Jämtlandsvaev) drafts for elaborate symmetrical patterns, symmetrically woven. For the American way of weaving crackle, warp-weft balance need not be a concern. The chief design advantage is beautiful color blendings and gentle movement of the dominant color from block to block according to the pattern the weaver desires.

Draft 69 is a crackle arrangement from the small profile of the time-

Draft 69

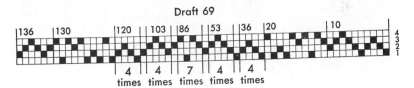

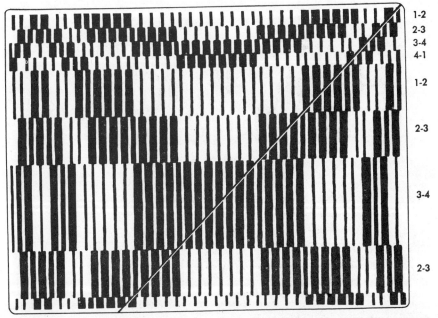

A crackle draft based on a seven-block diamond, with thread-by-thread development.

worn pattern known as Honeysuckle. The woven-as-drawn-in development shows the exact thread arrangement when crackle is woven with an alternating tabby. Pattern weft is held down by every fourth warp thread so that there are no floats longer than three threads. This development illustrates the peculiarity of this two-texture weave, which is that two blocks always weave as pattern and the remaining two as background. There is no way to avoid this comradeship of blocks except to omit drafting one block, as was done in draft 73 (page 130). When block A is woven, Block D weaves with it; when B is woven, A weaves with it; C carries B with it; and D, C.

It is possible to use the block comradeship advantageously by drafting crackle on opposites through omitting block B between A and C, omitting C between B and D, and so on. The diamond on opposites drafted at 70 shows how this is done. Notice that whenever a block is omitted it must

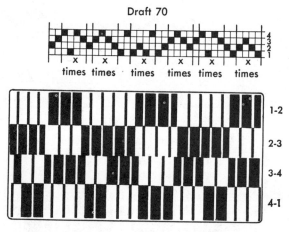

A crackle draft adapted from the opposites diamond.

still be recognized by including its transition thread. Drafts 71 and 72 are formal patterns which incorporate the opposites principle.

Perhaps the most interesting of all crackle patterns comes from the threading of large A, B, C, and D blocks to divide the warp into four equal areas. The eight diagrams accompanying draft 73 (page 130) indicate the modernistic effect of the designs which result. These, like other crackle patterns, are easily copied by eye through comparing the diagram with the developing weaving. The blocks are always so large and stylized that there is no difficulty in using this visual method, while following written direc-

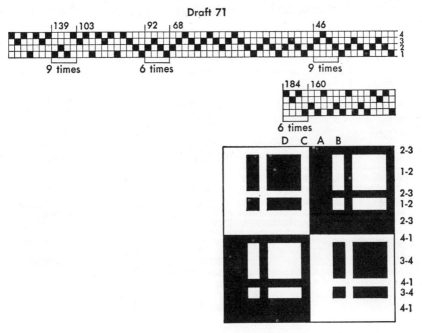

A crackle pattern on opposites.

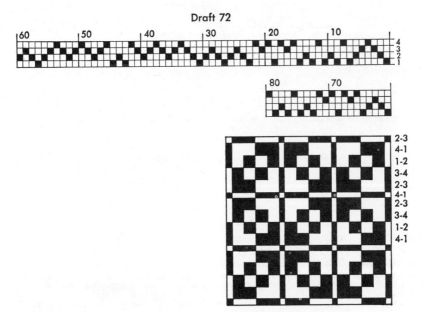

A crackle pattern on opposites, by Mary M. Atwater.

Draft 73

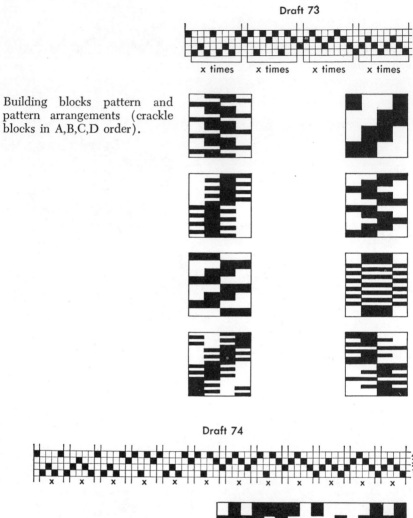

Building blocks pattern and pattern arrangements (crackle blocks in A,B,C,D order).

Draft 74

Lattice, a crackle pattern developed from overshot draft 42.

tions is slow, subject to error, and unimaginative. Another interesting classic draft is Lattice, draft 74. The origin of this draft is in the simple overshot twill blocks, draft 42 (page 106). If only the transition threads are read, one finds this twelve-thread overshot draft.

Weavers frequently need a stylized tree design for a decorative wall panel or runner. The traditional Pine Tree borders of colonial coverlets were woven in eight-harness summer-and-winter and are beyond the capacity of most looms. The problem of designing stylized trees on four

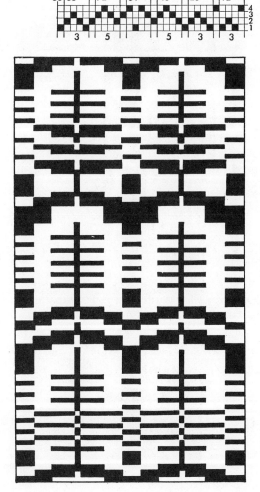

Arboretum, a crackle pattern for weaving stylized tree and shrub forms.

harnesses can be met only with a crackle draft; an attractive one is given in draft 75. Three different tree styles from this draft are shown on the diagram, but the imaginative weaver after copying these will be able to devise other tree forms.

For ecclesiastical weaving a cross design is often desirable and crackle proves an effective medium for this form, as shown in draft 76. The crosses

Draft 76

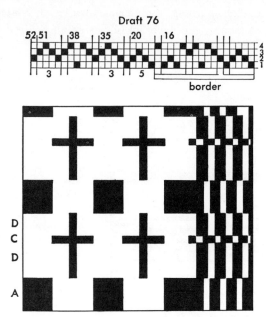

A crackle pattern for ecclesiastical uses.

may be drafted in any desired size by increasing the number of repeats in the B,C,B part of the design, but good proportions indicate that B should be three times the size of C, and five times the size of C is a good proportion for the separating square. The border may be threaded or not, as one wishes, and it may be added at the top and bottom by treadling A,C,D, in repeat. Trees and crosses are most effectively woven in the overshot method with a binder, and it is not necessary to obey the balance rule of placing as many tabby weft shots per inch as there are warp ends.

◄ ► THE UNIT CLASS

Although the actual textile types found in the *unit class* vary widely, all the threadings share important technical characteristics. The unit systems are all drafted without exceptions, overlaps, accidentals, transition threads, or other irregularities. All unit systems may be threaded from profile drafts by substitution of a key unit characteristic of the system. Each system has its own unit key, a static group of threads varying only in pattern block placement, which is substituted in the pattern squares of the profile. Each system also has its characteristic tie-up and treadling sequence. There are more individual systems within the unit class than in any other class, but many of them are weaves requiring more that four harnesses, or are obscure weaves of interest to the advanced weaver only.

Three members of the unit class are taken up here, three weaves which differ greatly in characteristics but which have in common the regularity of their draft systems and the fact that each is composed of threads placed on foundation harnesses to weave the base fabric and other threads on pattern harnesses to control placement of pattern blocks. In all three weaves two harnesses are required for the foundation, so that patterns with A and B blocks only may be used on a four-harness loom. As with other unit weaves further pattern complication requires more harnesses.

Drafts 77 through 88 are all profiles. This means that they serve as

133

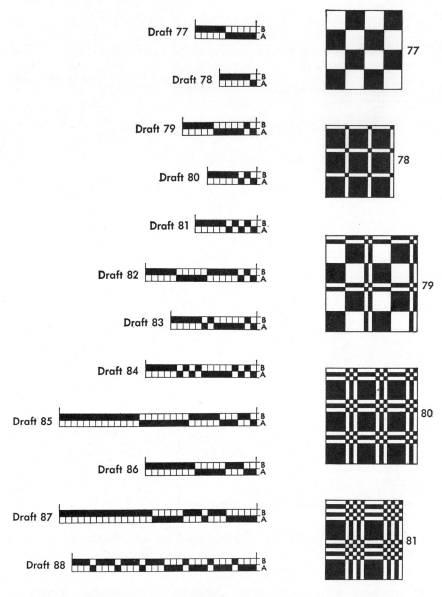

Two-block profile patterns. Substitution drafts for unit weaves such as summer-and-winter, Atwater-Bronson lace, and warp pattern.

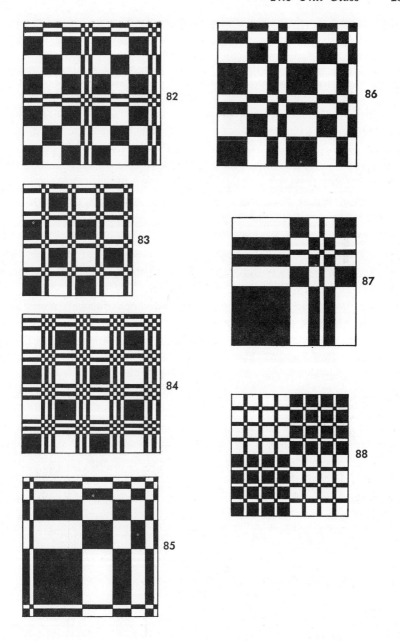

guides for the pattern arrangement but do not show placement of individual threads. Each square of a profile draft represents a single threading unit; the appropriate unit must be substituted for the square in the actual threading. The number of threads in the unit varies with the individual system, the summer-and-winter having a four-thread unit, Atwater-Bronson a six-thread unit, and warp pattern a three-thread unit. To thread draft 79, for instance, regardless of the system being used, the group of threads comprising the A unit is threaded first, then the B group; then follow five repeats of the A group and five repeats of the B group; then the whole thing is repeated. Thus, though the profile draft has only twelve squares, the actual threading of it in summer-and-winter requires forty-eight warp ends, in Atwater-Bronson sixty warp ends.

Accompanying each profile draft is a profile development of the woven-as-drawn-in pattern. All the patterns are unbalanced as they appear in full repeats. To complete the arrangement of any one of them for threading (unless for some reason the asymmetrical pattern is desired) one must break the pattern into two motifs and repeat the first motif at the end to balance the design. Another method for balancing a pattern, one which adds complication to some of the arrangements, is to use the last block as a return block and make the repeat in reverse direction.

The Summer-and-Winter System

Summer-and-winter is easy to understand because of its regularity and freedom from exceptions. The threading key, or substitution units for both blocks, is given below. The standard sinking-shed tie-up is at (a). The full tie-up at (b), and the skeleton tie-up at (c) for rising-shed indicate that though summer-and-winter can be woven on a counterbalanced loom, its full expression is attained only on a jack loom. The draft unit has four

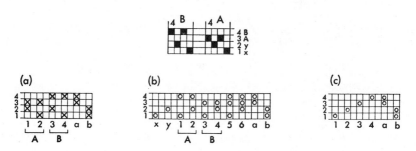

Summer-and-winter threading key and tie-ups.

threads, the first of which is known as tie-down x on harness 1, and the third tie-down y on harness 2. Full designing freedom requires that one be able to operate these tie-downs independently. The second and fourth threads of the unit are on one or the other pattern harness, block A formed by harness 3 and block B by harness 4. The two pattern harnesses combine to form the a tabby and the two tie-downs the b tabby. When a pattern harness is raised alone, weft floats entirely across all areas threaded to the opposite block. Therefore, to tie the pattern weft into the fabric a tie-down harness lifting every fourth thread must be raised with a pattern harness. When a tie-down harness is raised alone, the entire warp weaves in the pattern texture. When a tie-down harness is lifted with tabby a, background texture weaves across the entire warp.

The skeleton tie-up is a common convention for summer-and-winter and for other weaves which utilize more sheds than there are treadles. Each harness is tied individually to a treadle, in left to right order, and the tabbies are tied as usual to the two treadles at the far right. Pattern combinations are made by operating two or three treadles together. Adjacent combinations may be operated with one foot, or two feet for separated treadles. Thus it is possible to make all the fourteen four-harness sheds on only six treadles.

The many ways to weave summer-and-winter, each one producing a different texture, give it a versatility that makes this one of the most useful techniques. There are four different classic textures, each one achieved by a different treadling sequence and each one based on an exact balance between warp and tabby weft. The different textures do not harmonize well and therefore they cannot be combined in the same fabric.

The first method is in the overshot manner with tabby and pattern weft alternating, illustrated at (a) in the photograph on page 138. A single tie-down, which may be either x or y, is used, so that the two pattern blocks are woven with treadles 1 and 3, or 2 and 4. The sequence is:

Block A—treadle a, tabby weft	Block B—treadle a, tabby weft
" 1, pattern weft	" 3, pattern weft
" b, tabby weft	" b, tabby weft
" 1, pattern weft	" 3, pattern weft
repeat.	repeat.

Tie-down x makes each threaded unit stand out independently as at the top of each block at (a) in the photograph on page 138, while tie-down y creates an extra unit as shown in the lower halves of the blocks, and the edge units have two-thread instead of three-thread floats.

(a) Single tie-down method, *x* tie-down at top of blocks, *y* tie-down at bottom.

(b) Alternate tie-down method.

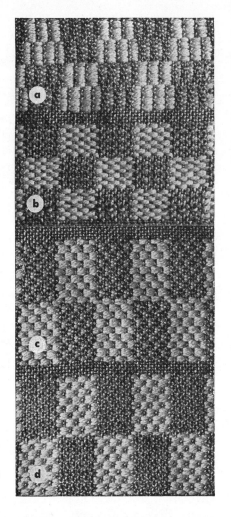

(c) The *x-y-y-x* method starting on tabby *b*.

(d) The *x-y-y-x* method starting on tabby *a*.

The classic summer-and-winter textures.

The second method illustrated at (b) in the photograph uses alternating tie-downs, so that all four pattern treadles are employed in the following sequence:

Block A—treadle a, tabby weft
       "   1, pattern weft
       "   b, tabby weft
       "   2, pattern weft
      repeat.

Block B—treadle a, tabby weft
       "   3, pattern weft
       "   b, tabby weft
       "   4, pattern weft
      repeat.

The third method (c in the photograph) produces one of the most beautiful textures known and is one of the most complex of treadling sequences. This method requires absolute precision, as an error in a single shot will alter the entire texture of the fabric, thereby ruining it. The textures are quite different on top and underneath and both are beautiful; so either side may be considered the right one—one side for winter and the other for summer, if you like. The classic double tie-down texture is woven in eight-shot sequences and each eight-thread sequence unit of four tabby shots and four pattern weft shots must exactly balance four warp ends. This means that the interweaving is very close, making this one of the strongest, firmest fabrics. The sequence is:

Block A—treadle b, tabby weft			Block B—treadle b, tabby weft	
"	2, pattern weft	(y)	"	4, pattern weft
"	a, tabby		"	a, tabby
"	1, pattern	(x)	"	3, pattern
"	b, tabby		"	b, tabby
"	1, pattern	(x)	"	3, pattern
"	a, tabby		"	a, tabby
"	2, pattern	(y)	"	4, pattern
repeat.			repeat.	

Reverse the tabby relationships (start with the *a* tabby and use the treadles in x, y, y, x order) to weave the underneath texture on top.

The fourth method, illustrated by (d), uses the (c) pattern-treadle or tie-down order but reverses the tabby relationship. Actually there are four different double-tie textures but two always occur together as top and bottom.

A further treadling which gives very modern effects and is never found among the classic weaves, though it is fairly common in primitive weaving, is the no-tabby summer-and-winter sequence. The four pattern treadles are used in 1, 2, 3, 4, repeat order without interruption. Many unique effects may be gained through using two or more colors in synchronized and progressing fashion with this treadling, and through using wefts of contrasting textures and sizes. This is a fruitful weave for experimenting for color and texture effects rather than pattern.

Summer-and-winter is the richest of all weaves for the experimenter. The reason for this lies in its close interweaving, the controls one can exert through the two tie-downs, and the independent nature of the two pattern blocks with their ability to combine for full pattern texture. The full background texture also helps increase the versatility.

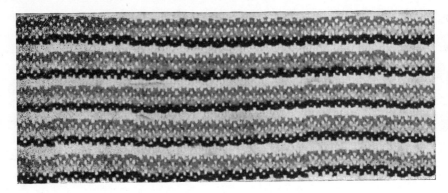

The no-tabby twill sequence method for weaving summer-and-winter, shown with four colors, four shots of each.

The Atwater-Bronson Lace System

This is the ever popular lace weave which modern handweavers probably use more than any other weave for linens. It is equally adaptable for use with wools, cottons, and synthetics.

Atwater-Bronson is a single-shuttle, balanced weave having two textures, an open lacy texture in which six warp and six weft threads group to form open spaces and tabby areas which contrast pleasantly with the open texture. Atwater-Bronson is seldom woven except in the classic manner. Its versatility lies in its adaptability to different materials and to a wide range of warp settings from very open to very dense. The lace texture has floats in both warp (wrong side) and weft (right side) over five ends, so that the maximum openness must be the practical five-thread float for the material being used. The limit for density is the closeness at which perfect tabby can be woven, and although very close settings lose the lacy openness, they develop a very deep texture which is remarkably beautiful.

Four-harness Atwater-Bronson threadings are made from two-block profiles and the lace effect is enhanced if no single-unit blocks are included. Each alternate thread of the entire draft is placed on harness 1, known as the tabby harness (the first, third and fifth threads of the six-thread unit) and every sixth thread (the last thread of the unit) is placed on harness 2, known as the tie-down harness. The remaining threads (the second and fourth of the unit) are placed on a pattern harness. The unit

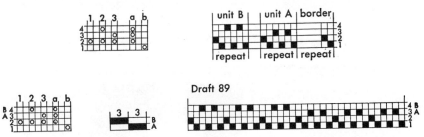

Draft 89

The Atwater-Bronson threading key and tie-up, with thread-by-thread draft.

key is shown above. Draft 89 shows a thread-by-thread draft as well as a profile. The scope of the system is enlarged by the fact that tabby stripes, borders, and selvages may be added by threading 1,2 alternately.

As this weave produces a tabby by raising harness 1 alone, the opposite tabby is formed by the pattern and tie-down harnesses. This unbalanced harness arrangement cannot easily be woven on a counterbalanced loom. One treadle is required for weaving each pattern block through tying to it the harness which is to weave as tabby background as well as the tie-down harness. The tie-down harness is operated alone to weave the lace texture across the entire pattern threading.

One popular design is especially adapted to the Atwater-Bronson system, the picture frame pattern, whereby a border may be woven around all four sides of an article such as a table mat, a head scarf, or a baby blanket. The two styles of picture-frame borders are shown at drafts 90 and 91 (page 142). The simple border illustrated in the photograph (page 143) is drafted at 90 and a more complex border with cross bars at 91. These two profiles have two peculiarities. There is an additional block indicated at each side, under the block A draft line. This is the wide band of tabby which is threaded 1, 2 alternately. Second, the block sizes and proportions are implied but are not given specifically. The reason for this is that both of these designs must be adapted to the number of threads in the specific warp and also to the width of the border, relative to the tabby edge and to the tabby center. Picture frame designs are woven on two pattern treadles. The horizontal border, having no tabby background except that threaded on 1,2 alternately, weaves when one raises the tie-down harness alone. The side borders, which are threaded as block A on harness 3 and have B areas woven as tabby background, weave on the treadle which raises harness 4 plus the tie-down.

Draft 90

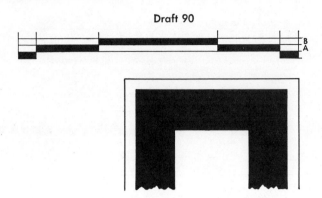

Profile draft for simple picture frame.

Draft 91

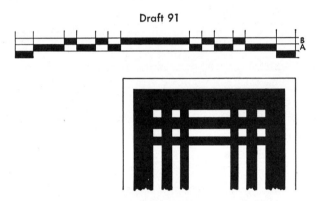

Profile draft for cross-barred "picture frame."

The Atwater-Bronson system may be employed for weaving crosses in a lightweight single-weft fabric, and so the system is a favorite for ecclesiastical linens. Crosses either large or small are drafted on the two pattern blocks and spaces between the crosses are threaded 1, 2 alternately. Thus, a linen may be threaded with a large cross in the center, with a small cross in each corner, or with a repeat arrangement of allover crosses. These arrangements are shown in drafts 92, 93, and 94 (page 144).

The Atwater-Bronson treadling is in a six-shot sequence which is comparable to the six-thread draft unit. It is tabby *b*, pattern, tabby *b*, pattern,

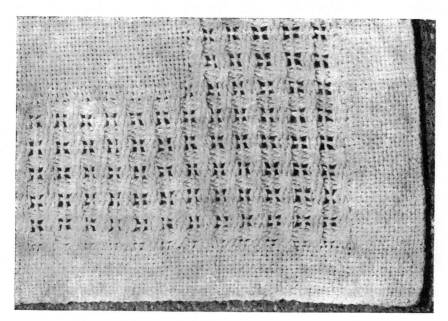

Corner of "picture-frame" mat in Atwater-Bronson lace.

tabby *b*, tabby *a*. For the pattern one may use treadle 1 (the tie-down alone), which weaves lace texture in both pattern blocks; treadle 2 (tied to harnesses 2 and 4), which weaves lace in A areas, tabby in B areas; treadle 3 (tied to harnesses 2 and 3), which weaves lace in the B areas, tabby in the A. Notice the characteristic which applies to other weaves in which the pattern floats are of weft, that raised pattern harnesses weave their areas as background, unmoved harnesses weave their areas as pattern texture. Great care must be taken to beat Atwater-Bronson for an exact balance, and the weaving of the full lace texture requires particular restraint since there are no tabby areas to provide resistance to weft packing.

The effect gained by this weave is at its best when warp and weft are identical in both thread and color. This is very definitely a single-color weave and even the use of two closely associated values of the same color detracts from rather than enhances the beauty of the texture. Sometimes a contrasting thread is placed on harness 2 (each sixth thread) and woven on tabby *a* (each sixth shot), and metallic in this position adds a pleasant glitter.

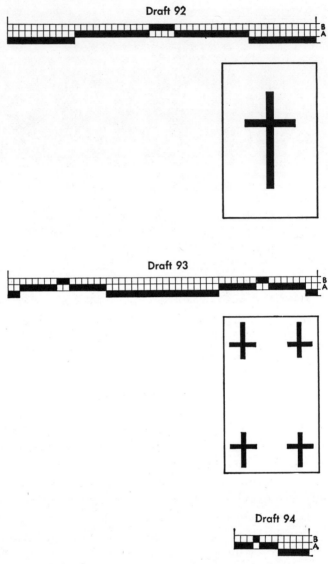

Atwater-Bronson lace drafts of ecclesiastical weaving.

The Warp Pattern System

This is a tabby foundation weave in which patterns are formed through extra warp threads instead of by the more usual means of pattern weft. Although allover patterns may be woven in this system, and frequently

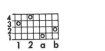

Warp-pattern threading keys and tie-up.

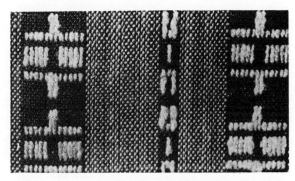

Warp pattern stripes, from draft 96 (page 146).

are in the multiple-harness interpretations, four-harness *warp pattern* is usually used for designed pattern stripes.

There are two types of threading used for making warp pattern borders, both shown in their key units above. Both utilize a foundation fabric of tabby, threaded on harnesses 1, 2 alternately, and pattern threads placed on harnesses 3 and 4 to form simple designs. The first method, (a), used in the photographed sample, threads two base tabby ends followed by a single pattern warp end in a three-thread unit. The second, (b), has a more closely set pattern warp with a pattern warp thread alternating with each base tabby in a four-thread unit. A special sleying method is practical for this weave. Sley the entire tabby fabric at one per dent or two per dent, according to the design plan, and tie in the base warp. Then sley the pattern threads, adding threads to already sleyed dents according to the pattern arrangement (with base warp sleyed 2 per dent, the pattern stripes are sleyed 3 per dent for the three-thread unit, 4 per dent for the four-thread unit). The pattern, it is clear, is composed of superficial decorative threads which form design rather than fabric.

There is a certain problem in the beaming of a warp which contains added pattern stripes. If not handled carefully, the warp will build up at the places where the extra pattern warp occurs and destroy the tension. For short warps, this may be obviated by using very substantial beam padding such as a continuous roll of corrugated cardboard or many lease sticks. For long warps it is advisable to beam the pattern warp on a second beam, if such is available, or even on a separate loom. But there is another method which is altogether practical; this involves beaming the base warp alone and winding each pattern warp stripe in a separate chain. The pattern warp chains are then hung individually over the back beam and supplied with suitable weights to give adequate tension. If each is unchained to within a few inches of the floor and hung with a weight at that position, weaving may progress until the weights reach the back beam before the pattern warp need be readjusted.

Profile drafts and a few designs for warp pattern stripes.

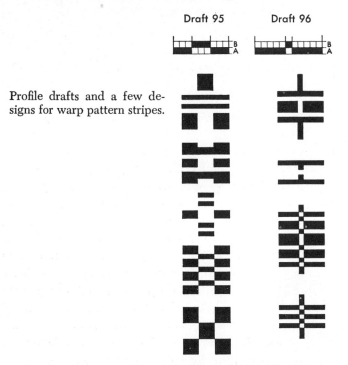

Draft 95   Draft 96

Drafts 95 and 96 show suggested pattern stripe arrangements, and under these are several patterns from the many which may be woven on each. Any two-block profile may be used as the threading draft.

▶ THE GROUPED
THREAD CLASS

The weaves of the *grouped thread* class are often known as linen weaves because of their traditional use for household linens. All of them alternate tabby areas with texture spots. All are balanced weaves for which warp and weft should be identical. They are also single-color weaves, but often the visual depth of the texture areas may be increased by using one color for warp and a different though close value of the same color for weft. Though they are first of all considered linen weaves, the grouped thread systems are excellent for wool and may be used for cotton, silk, or any of the synthetics.

The Huck System

Classic huck is the single simple draft 97 (page 148). It weaves to an allover texture which is firm but soft and absorbent. The curving of both warp and weft threads which occurs when tension is released and the fabrics have been washed is a delightful feature. Variations of the draft may be made by using three-thread or seven-thread units instead of the more usual five-thread unit. Tabby for selvages, borders, and plain stripes is threaded on harnesses 1, 4 alternately.

Huck is woven in a shed sequence which resembles the draft units: *a*, 1, *a*, 1, *a*; *b*, 2, *b*, 2, *b*; repeated continuously. This weaves the classic

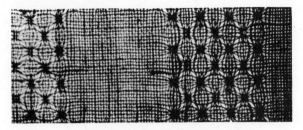

Huck stripes with tabby between.

Draft 97

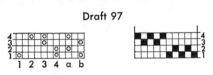

The basic huck draft and tie-up.

texture which is huck, but treadle 3 may be tied to 1-2 and treadles 3 to 3-4 for creating special effects and borders.

Since huck is a closely interwoven fabric with curved threads and has no pattern in the general sense, it is a good foundation threading for special effects in textiles using unconventional materials and combinations of materials and colors.

The Spot Bronson System

The *spot Bronson* is a classic linen weave used by our forefathers for handspun linen towels and table linens.

Each alternate thread of the draft is on harness 1 and the intermediate threads are placed in pairs on the other three harnesses to control design. Like other linen weaves, it has a perfect warp-weft balance, utilizes identical material for warp and weft, and is best if woven in a single color or in two closely associated values of a color. The draft unit has four threads, which through an overlap, group into five-thread spots with two floats. Though somewhat resembling huck, spot Bronson differs from it in that two-thirds of the texture is tabby instead of one-half, the warp and weft threads curve less, and the system has more design potential since it is possible to draft three spot-units on four harnesses. Various arrangements of the three pattern units may be made, but the designing is limited by the fact that no unit may be repeated to form a block. Draft 98 shows a typical arrangement in which two units alternate for a certain distance in

Draft 98

Spot Bronson table with separating unit.

Draft 99

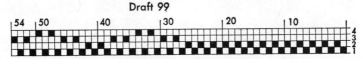

Spot Bronson tabby stripes alternated.

Draft 100

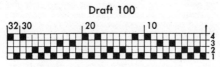

Spot Bronson diamond.

a table-like motif, separated by the third unit. Draft 99 shows the A unit repeated for twenty-six ends. In a draft of such character, the A unit is used to form tabby and cannot be woven as a texture spot, but B and C are grouped to form small spot motifs completely surrounded by tabby.

The treadling is simple, a four-shot sequence similar to the threading units. The sequence is

Unit A—tabby b	Unit B—tabby b	Unit C—tabby b
pattern 1	pattern 2	pattern 3
tabby b	tabby b	tabby b
pattern 1.	pattern 2.	pattern 3.

The *a* treadle is used only when alternated with *b* to weave plain tabby.

Modern variations in this weave vary the block sizes but place the weft in classic sequences. An interesting variation is achieved through threading a different type of material on the tabby harness from that used on the pattern harnesses. This is another weave which is so simple that it is an excellent foundation for experiments in texture and color effects.

The M's and O's System

M's and O's, though not as versatile nor as generally practical a weave as huck or spot Bronson, should not be omitted from a treatment of the grouped thread class or the classic linen weaves. M's and O's can produce a beautiful fabric, even though more often than not it is so poorly handled that its beauty is questionable. The importance of the weave lies in the fact that it is balanced and therefore the only one of the common linen

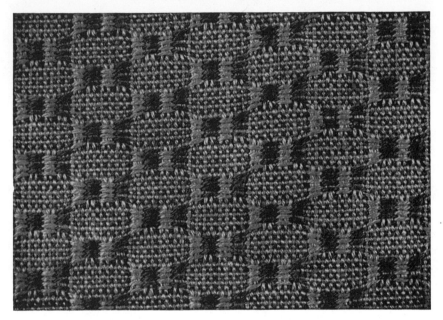

M's and O's from draft 101, woven with alternating colors.

weaves which may be done conveniently on a counterbalanced loom. A balanced weave of identical warp and weft, it has texture blocks of four-thread opposite floats, which should weave as weft rep, contrasted to intermediate tabby blocks. This difficult texture combination requires an unusually closely set warp and a very sharp beat, and also limits the vertical development of the texture blocks to avoid their becoming sleazy at the top. Because large blocks have a tendency to become soft, spongy and stringy looking, they are better avoided and the drafting and weaving restricted to small pattern areas. Draft 101 is the simple, alternate texture arrangement repeating the two eight-thread units. Draft 102 shows a different way for handling the two design units.

The weave will not produce a tabby, even though the intermediate blocks weave as tabby. The selvage threading is 1, 4 repeated, and this threading may be used to introduce tabby stripes into the pattern. An in-

Draft 101

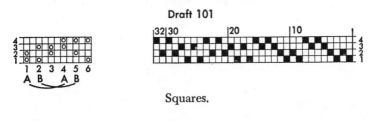

Squares.

Draft 102

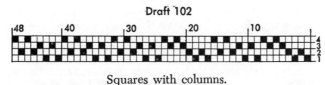

Squares with columns.

Draft 103

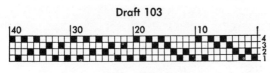

Squares with tabby tie-down.

Basic drafts for M's and O's with tie-up.

teresting drafting variation is the placing of a 1, 4 threading between each pattern block as is done in draft 103. Pattern blocks always have an eight-thread grouping: 1,2,1,2;3,4,3,4, which may be repeated, for A; 1,3,1,3; 2,4,2,4, which may be repeated, for B.

M's and O's is woven on the opposites principle, using the balanced tie-up as given with draft 101. Block A areas are woven by alternating treadles 1 and 4 (1-2 and 3-4) and Block B areas by alternating treadles 2 and 5 (1-3 and 2-4). Treadles 3 and 6 (2-3 and 4-1) are not used in weaving classic M's and O's, but they are useful when this threading system is used as a foundation for fabrics of a free texture weave. It is plain that the weaving may be accomplished on the standard tie-up by alternating treadles 1,3 for A and *a, b* for B.

THE DOUBLE
WEAVE CLASS

The four-harness *double weave* has many useful applications, since it produces simultaneously two independent tabby fabrics which may be of different colors and even of different materials. The two surfaces of plain double weave fabrics may be woven completely independently or they may be joined at one side or at both sides. When joined at one side only, the result is a single fabric twice the warp width. When joined at both sides, the result is a seamless tubing. Or it is possible to interchange the surfaces of the two fabrics in horizontal stripes which join the fabrics horizontally wherever the surface interchange takes place. The imaginative weaver finds many uses for the double weave.

Draft 104

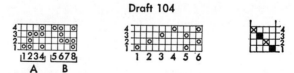

Draft and tie-up for single-alternation double weave.

Double fabrics are woven on a four-harness twill threading. If surfaces of two different colors or two different yarns are desired, thread one material on the odd-numbered harnesses and the other on the even-num-

Draft 105

A   B

Draft and tie-up for paired-alternation double weave.

bered ones so that the two threads alternate throughout. The double weave tie-up is the skeleton tie-up for six treadles, one to attach to each harness and two to form the *a* (2-4) and *b* (1-3) tabby sheds. Draft 104 shows the threading and tie-up. Plainly this is another weave for the jack loom. A second threading places one color on harnesses 1 and 2, the other on 3 and 4, as on draft and tie-up 105.

Since two fabrics are woven simultaneously, the warp sett should be twice as close as the normal tabby. The best sley is four threads per dent.

The principle of the double weave is that one tabby fabric is woven on the odd-numbered harnesses at the same time another tabby fabric is woven under it on the even-numbered harnesses. To weave the top fabric one need merely alternate harnesses 1 and 3, while all threads carried on harnesses 2 and 4 float uninvolved under the surface. To weave the under fabric it is necessary to get the top fabric out of the way by raising harnesses 1 and 3, and then treadle sheds 2 and 4 alternately. Since the beat would be interferred with if either surface were built up independently for any distance, smooth weaving requires alternate shots on the top and bottom surfaces, or at least alternate pairs of shots. For draft 104 the tabby treadles are used to raise an entire surface and hold it out of the way while the under surface is being woven, rather than to make weaving sheds. Treadles raising 1-2 and 3-4 do this for draft 105.

Supposing a warp of light threads on harnesses 1 and 3, dark on 2 and 4, woven with two shuttles carrying light and dark weft, the treadling with draft and tie-up 104 is as follows:

Light surface on top:

(a)	Or	(b)
treadle 1, light;		treadle 1, light;
" *b* and 2 (1-2-3), dark;		" 3, light;
" 3, light;		" *b* and 2 (1-2-3), dark;
" *b* and 4 (1-3-4), dark;		" *b* and 4 (1-3-4), dark;
repeat.		repeat.

Dark surface on top:

(a)	Or	(b)
treable 2, dark;		treadle 2, dark;
" *a* and 1 (1-2-4), light;		" 4, dark;
" 4, dark;		" *a* and 1 (1-2-4), light;
" *a* and 3 (2-3-4), light;		" *a* and 3 (2-3-4), light;
repeat.		repeat.

If desired, the edges may be closed by locking the two wefts after each shot in the manner used to make good edges for any two-shuttle weave. The surfaces may be separated and padding inserted between them before they are permanently closed through interchange of surfaces, by raising the appropriate tabby treadle, 1-3 for light on top, 2-4 for dark on top.

Double-width fabric is produced by using a single shuttle with either of the (b) treadle sequences. Seamless tubing is woven by using either of the (a) sequences with a single shuttle. However, on a warp with alternating colors a different shed sequence is required for weaving a uniform fabric with alternating color on both sides. Harnesses 1 and 2 must be used for the top surface, and 3 and 4 for the under surface. The sequences then become:

(a)	Or	(b)
treadle 1,		treadle 1,
" *b* and 2 (1-2-3),		" 2,
" 2,		" *a* and 1 (1-2-4),
" *a* and 1 (1-2-4),		" *b* and 2 (1-2-3),
repeat.		repeat.

As above, (a) weaves the seamless tubing and (b) the double-width fabric, both with a single shuttle.

The simple block patterns characteristic of early colonial double-woven coverlets require multiple harnesses. The elaborate double weave patterns seen in mid-nineteenth century coverlets are made on a Jacquard loom, while elaborate primitive and peasant patterns, as well as modern ones, are done by a complex pick-up method, directions for which are not in keeping with a book on weaving fundamentals.

The Double Face Twill Weave

Double face twill is a method for weaving 3/1 twill fabrics of one color on one side, another color on the other side, a common blanket technique.

Although the same six-treadle tie-up is used for the double weave, the warp is set at a normal twill density. Two colors are selected for weft which may be different from the warp color, as the warp is almost hidden. The top surface is woven with one color in the 3/1 twill which raises one harness and permits the weft to float over three warp ends. The under surface, which is completely interwoven with the top surface, uses the second color and is in the 3/1 twill which raises three harnesses so that the weft floats over only one warp end. The two colors must be used alternately in the following sequence.

> treadle 1, dark weft;
> " b and 2 (1-2-3), light weft;
> " 2, dark weft;
> " a and 1 (1-2-4), light weft;
> " 3, dark weft;
> " b and 4 (1-3-4), light weft;
> " 4, dark weft;
> " a and 3 (2-3-4), light weft;
> repeat.

◀◀
▶ THE RHYTHMIC
WEAVE CLASS

This is a catch-all class containing a number of rather obscure and un-related weave systems. The only characteristic these weaves share is that they do not follow the rules for any other classes, but in each the thread-ing is based on a rhythmic sequence characteristic of itself only. There is one very important weave in this class, the *shadow weave,* and a minor one, the *blanket weave,* which have appropriate places in this study.

The Shadow Weave System

Shadow weave may be compared to the two-harness log cabin, as it consists of pattern blocks formed of alternating light and dark threads lying either horizontally or vertically, exactly as in log cabin. But there are four pattern blocks, and in arrangement these resemble crackle since com-panion blocks weave together, two blocks weaving in horizontal pin stripes and the remaining two in vertical pin stripes, and adjacent blocks have a complete overlap.

The threading requires that light and dark threads alternate throughout. Block shifts are formed by harness threading shifts, without alteration of the color sequence. Block A has dark on harness 1, light on 3; B has dark

Shadow weave double diamond, draft 108.

Draft 106

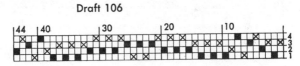

Shadow weave, irregular diamond.

Draft 107

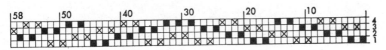

Shadow weave, large diamond.

Draft 108

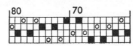

Shadow weave, double diamond.

on 2, light on 4; C has dark on 3, light on 1; D has dark on 4, light on 2. Treadling is done on the four pattern sheds of the standard tie-up, with treadles used in an opposite rhythm which duplicates the threading system. Thus, block A is woven by throwing dark weft in shed 1, light in 3 and repeating as desired; block B has dark in shed 2, light in 4, repeated; C has dark on 3, light on 1; D has dark on 4, light on 2.

The shadow weave fabric is tabby except at the block edges where two-thread floats form interesting light and dark outlines for the blocks. Because of the very close weaving of the near-tabby, shadow weave is an excellent technique for lightweight fabrics, particularly light woolens and worsteds. It weaves to a handsome, rather subtle fabric if threaded and woven in all one color. Interesting color effects are gained by using weft colors different from the warp colors. The tabby dominance might make this seem to be an excellent weave for linens, but this is not generally the case. Since the effect is one of alternating colors and colors do not blend well in linen, only through extensive sampling is it possible to create a good linen effect in shadow weave.

The blanket weave, draft 109.

The Blanket Weave System

The *blanket weave* is an odd and little known weave that forms a firm but soft fabric suitable for certain types of drapery and for blankets; it

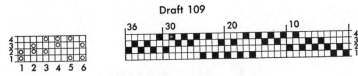

Draft 109

A diamond in blanket weave.

makes charming baby blankets. The patterns resemble overshot woven on the opposites principle except that there are six rather than four blocks and the interlacement does not form a tabby. The blocks are the four drafted for overshot plus two additional ones which alternate the even-numbered harnesses and the odd-numbered ones. Because of the peculiar overlap caused by the insertion of these last two blocks, half of the blocks are composed of even numbers of threads and half of odd numbers. Diamond patterns draft most effectively and the extra blocks must be placed between B and C and between D and A, in the order shown in the draft, if a smooth pattern flow is to be attained. Otherwise the pattern is confused with awkward opposites. The draft shows all blocks of four- and five-thread size, and patterns are usually more effective if the block size is kept uniform, but they may be six and seven threads, or seven and eight, and so on. This is not a balanced weave and warp is usually fine and set about twice as wide as for twill. Two colors of weft, heavier than the warp, are used alternately. The tie-up for the six treadles follows the harness combinations of the blocks. Treadling is on opposites (alternate treadles 1 and 4, 2 and 5, 3 and 6, 4 and 1, 5 and 2, 6 and 3) with a light weft in one shed and a dark in the other to create two interlacing pattern figures, one of light and one of dark. Blocks are built up as desired, since this weave has no balance rules.

▶ WEAVING
METHODS

Single-Shuttle Weaving

Beyond stressing rhythm in all the motions of weaving, there would be little to say about a weave as obvious as tabby were it not for the fact that tabby combines with pattern in two-shuttle pattern weaves. To form the right weaving habits so that a tabby error can never occur in a two-shuttle weave, there is one unbreakable rule to follow. When the shuttle is in the left hand, ready to pass from left to right, always press the *a* or left tabby treadle. When the shuttle is in the right hand, ready to travel from right to left, always press the *b* or right tabby treadle. This rule holds true whether the tabby treadles are being operated in walking-motion or with the right foot only.

Two-Shuttle Weaving

To weave two-shuttle pattern systems, follow the rule given above for the tabby direction. The rule for pattern direction is that the pattern shuttle follows the tabby, and in the same direction.

Weft locking at selvages is important for making good edges. The lock is accomplished by laying shuttles down in the same relative positions after shots. Common practice is to lay one shuttle on the textile and then pick up the other one for the next shot. If the tabby shuttle is always placed toward the beater and the pattern shuttle toward the weaver, the wefts automatically lock. The lock occurs for the reverse order too. The important point is to be consistent.

The same rules hold true for two-shuttle opposites weaving.

Three-Shuttle Weaving—The Italian Method

When weaving with three shuttles, it is advisable to place a small table at each side of the loom to hold the shuttles. Three wefts are locked by laying the shuttles down always in the same order.

The most important three-shuttle weave is known, for some obscure reason, as the Italian method. This is the method given in detail under the crackle weave as the classic method for weaving crackle. It may also be used as a no-tabby method for overshot, and is a good sequence to try when experimenting with other threadings with four pattern treadles. Some find the weaving easier if four shuttles are used in the manner given below, with two shuttles carrying identical weft.

Four-Shuttle Weaving—Bound Weaving

When weaving with four shuttles, the pair of loom-side tables is necessary. In classic four-shuttle weaves, the shuttles follow each other in sequence and it is imperative that wefts be locked at the edge through the shuttle order. The best system is to start all wefts at one side. As each shuttle is caught on the opposite side, lay it down in back of the previous shuttle until the four lie in a row. Then pick up the front shuttle to throw. It often happens that two threads of the same color occur in the four-weft sequences. If trouble is to be avoided, do not throw both shots with the same shuttle. Put bobbins of the same weft in two (or three, if necessary) shuttles and retain the shuttle order.

Bound weaving is four-shuttle weaving with no tabby, in which the four pattern treadles are operated in 1, 2, 3, 4, order. Classically the weave uses a weft as fine as the warp, or finer, and the fabric is beaten to give a full warp coverage in a weft rep. The weft must be extremely loose in the shed and is usually placed in a wide curving arc from selvage to selvage, sometimes "bubbled" down into scallops all across the warp with the index finger. Patterns in bound weaving are made by shifting the color order through picking up the front shuttle and moving it to the back

Sampler woven on draft 44. *Top border:* two-shuttle opposites method. *Second border:* four-shuttle bound method. *Third border:* three-shuttle crackle method. *Others:* patterns in bound method.

where it will weave fourth instead of first, or by rearranging shuttles in some other systematic way. Colors may be added and subtracted at will, but never more than four can be in use at one time. The fabric has a right and a wrong side.

The No-Tabby Sequence Weave

The no-tabby sequences are generally woven on the four summer-and-winter pattern treadles, but they can be used with some other systems. Pattern treadles are operated in 1, 2, 3, 4, order, without interruption, but with more interpretive freedom than for classic bound weaving. For summer-and-winter, the colors are usually used in pairs of shots, and one of the more interesting color sequences uses three colors in pair rotation. Weft the same as the warp or much heavier than the warp may be used; in fact, almost any kind of weft is suitable, right down to sticks and grasses. This is a free weave, one for the imaginative weaver.

Opposites Weaving

Opposites may be woven, without tabby, on overshot, crackle, summer-and-winter, and certain other threadings. The rule of opposites is that all four harnesses must be involved once in two treadle tie-ups, so that the two treadles compensate each other. For overshot threadings and the standard tie-up treadles 1 and 3 are opposites, and treadles 2 and 4, just as the *a* and *b* tabbys are opposites. By using these in alternate order, with a dark weft in one shed, a light in the other and weaving any pair until a block is built up, unusual texture and pattern effects are achieved. The best opposites weaving uses a soft weft beaten to form a strong weft emphasis.

Honeycomb

Honeycomb is a special effect, sometimes called overshot lace, usually woven on overshot threadings but very good on M's and O's. Honeycomb requires a very heavy weft of the same color as the warp, and a fine weft which may be in a contrasting color or value. The tie-up is made with harnesses 1-2-3 on treadle 1, 2-3-4 on 2, 1-3-4 on 3, 1-2-4 on 4, plus tabbies. To weave treadle: *a*, *b* with heavy weft; 1, 2, repeat as desired, with fine weft; *b*, *a* heavy weft; 2, 3, repeat, fine weft; *a*, *b* heavy weft; 3, 4, repeat, fine weft; *b*, *a* heavy weft; 4, 1, repeat, fine weft. The unusual requirement is that tabby treadles are used in *a*, *b*, then in *b*, *a* order, so that the same outline shot lies on both sides of any spot. The strongest honeycomb effects are made on two-block overshot opposites or M's and O's drafts with long

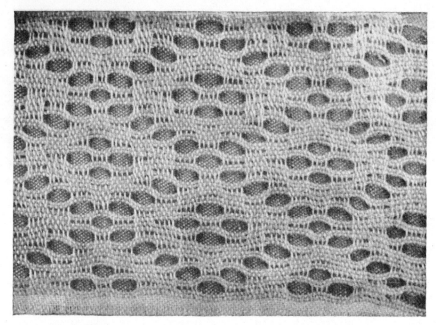

Honeycomb woven on a six-block overshot diamond.

blocks. For M's and O's the outline weft is thrown in the 3-4 and 4-1 sheds. The overshot honeycomb fabric has a definite right and wrong side.

The Swivel Weave

The swivel method uses the four pattern treadles in unbroken 1, 2, 3, 4, order, with the same unbalanced tie-up required by overshot honeycomb. Treadle 1 combines 1-2-3, treadle 2 is 2-3-4, treadle 3 is 1-3-4, treadle 4 is 1-2-4, with no tabbies. Weave with two colors, throwing pairs of shots with each color:

Block A—treadle 1, 2 with dark weft, treadle 3, 4 with light weft;
Block B—treadle 1 with light, 2, 3 with dark, 4 with light;
Block C—treadle 1, 2 with light, 3, 4 with dark;
Block D—treadle 1 with dark, 2, 3 with light, 4 with dark.

Use a fine or a soft weft which will beat to cover the warp.

▶ WEAVING SKILLS

Weaving is a rhythm, a rhythm which can carry much of the expressive feeling of dancing. For many, the highest pleasure can be attained from weaving only when the various movements of treadling, beating, shuttle-throwing, and shuttle-catching are so coordinated that they flow as if to music. Each of these movements plays an important part in the full weaving cycle.

Treadling

Treadling, to be rhythmic, must be in left-right walking order, at least as far as possible, and it must be by the touch system. The touch system is developed through making the tie-up so that treadles are operated by the left and right foot alternately. The standard tie-up does this for all tabby-foundation weaves derived from twills, and the characteristic tie-ups for most other weaves, as they are given here, are for walking order. For weaves which alternate tabby shots with pattern shots, including not only the two-shuttle pattern weaves but such single-shuttle weaves as Atwater-Bronson, and the grouped thread weaves, the convention of placing tabby treadles at the far right and pattern treadles at the left takes care of the walking order. Occasionally someone will challenge this order on the assumption that tabby is treadled more than any other weave and that therefore the tabby treadles should be tied in the center where they are most conveniently operated. An experienced weaver immediately sees the weakness of this contention, for the versatile weaver is able to treadle slightly off side as easily as in the center of the loom, and does not find it difficult to treadle *a* and *b* alternately with left and right foot, or 1 and 2 in the same manner. For a prolonged tabby project it is undeniably true that center tabbies are easier, but one should make a special tie-up for such projects, a tie-up not used for other weaves. Balanced twill on treadles 1, 2, 3, 4, repeated is an undeniably awkward operation on the standard tie-up, but the tie-up is easily arranged for efficient right-left treadling. Simply tie treadle 2 to 3-4 and treadle 3 to 2-3. Then weave 1, 3, 2, 4—left, right, left, right, continuously. Special touch-system tie-up and treadling methods are used for multiple-harness weaves with many treadles, but these need not be taken up here.

Shuttle Throwing

Shuttle throwing should be without awkwardness. No discussion of the right way to hold a shuttle is given here because weavers disagree on this subject and the truth seems to be that different people prefer different methods and use them with equal efficiency. It is sufficient to say that the shuttle must be held easily and lightly, so that it may be thrown the full distance of the shed without awkwardness or undue effort. It must be caught so that it may be rethrown with a flowing motion without a full change of hand position, and it should be caught in such a way that a finger is available to stop the spinning of the bobbin when this is necessary. The bobbin, while the shuttle is in motion, must give off weft sufficiently freely to prevent drag where the weft turns at the selvage and to allow the weft to lie on a loose diagonal in the shed without the slightest tension.

Beating

Perhaps the greatest skill of weaving lies in the beating. The beater should be held lightly between the fingers, instead of with a fist, and in the exact center. The throwing motion should be free, like that of a ball-player throwing a ball, as beating with tense muscles is fatiguing, destroys the weaving rhythm, and reduces the weaver's sensitivity to the feel of the warp as it slips through the reed, a sensitivity which is necessary for smooth and perfect weaving. The beater is thrown swiftly if the weave is firm, gently if it is soft.

Skillful combination of these three operations leads to rhythm and ultimately to good textiles. The coordination of the beat with treadling and shuttle throwing is a problem for many novices, who wonder if the beat should be a single or a double tap, if it should precede the shed change or follow it or both. The answer is that a good weaver must know how to beat in many ways, because different fabrics require different beats. The object of the beat is to place a loosely lying weft into the position the fabric requires. To do this the shed must be open as the reed carries the weft forward to the fell (the weaving line), since the tension of a changed shed prevents the weft from taking its natural position and may cause serious narrowing across the fabric. However, the open shed beat may not give the weft its correct position and so an additional beat may be required after the weft has been locked into position by the shed change. This gives a rhythm: treadle, beat, shuttle, beat; repeat. Sometimes this rhythm, even with a very fast, sharp beat, is not sufficient to place the weft close enough, in which case each beat may be a double tap. This extra beat is often needed with classic summer-and-winter or the overshot-twill hybrid. On the other hand, if a single beat is sufficient to place the weft correctly, the beat should be on the open shed in the order: treadle, shuttle, beat; repeat. This may be a double beat if needed. A very skillful weaver whose work has become completely rhythmic learns to make a single beat so coordinated with the shed change that the reed touches the fell at the exact instant the shed changes. This is probably the most efficient beat there is, especially for single-shuttle weaves. There are certain cases of extremely open warps for which it is difficult to place weft correctly owing to too little friction. Additional beat friction is gained for such warps by closing the shed (*not* changing the shed) and beating, or pressing the beater lightly with the full warp in the rest position.

A word more about rhythm. Rhythm is never achieved until the individual motions of the cycle are perfected and natural. Therefore weave very slowly at first, putting the effort on making all the motions economically. Maintain a perfect rhythm, no matter how slow, until the speed increases naturally through the body's familiarity with the motions. The motions will soon become unconscious responses.

▶ INDEX

169